CREATIVITY

IN THE ARTS

Edited by

VINCENT TOMAS

Brown University

CONTEMPORARY PERSPECTIVES
IN PHILOSOPHY SERIES

PRENTICE-HALL, INC. Englewood Cliffs, New Jersey

PRENTICE-HALL INTERNATIONAL, INC., *London*
PRENTICE-HALL OF AUSTRALIA, PTY., LTD., *Sydney*
PRENTICE-HALL OF CANADA, LTD., *Toronto*
PRENTICE-HALL FRANCE, S.A.R.L., *Paris*
PRENTICE-HALL OF INDIA (PRIVATE) LTD., *New Delhi*
PRENTICE-HALL OF JAPAN, INC., *Tokyo*
PRENTICE-HALL DE MEXICO, S.A., *Mexico City*

© 1964
by PRENTICE-HALL, INC.
Englewood Cliffs, N.J.

Second printing .... September, 1964

Library of Congress Catalog Card Number:
64-11552

Printed in the United States of America
C-19129

CONTEMPORARY PERSPECTIVES

IN PHILOSOPHY

This series is designed to provide a wide group of readers with collections of essays by contemporary philosophers on problems presently under active discussion in philosophical circles. The articles have been carefully selected for their lucidity and intelligibility, revealing the vitality of current philosophy to an audience which would not normally have recourse to professional journals. Each volume consists of articles devoted to a single topic, thereby creating an unusual degree of internal coherence and dialectical unity. In many cases the articles are addressed to one another as replies or rebuttals, or are otherwise built upon earlier essays to carry the discussion forward to new levels of clarity. The editor of each volume contributes an introduction which furnishes the reader with the orientation and general framework for a full understanding of the issues. Although each volume is deliberately restricted in scope, the series as a whole ranges over the entire breadth of philosophy, from aesthetics and philosophy of religion to semantics and philosophy of science.

The series is dedicated to the view that contemporary philosophical perspectives—even on ancient problems—are distinctive, exciting, and fully intelligible to students and other nonprofessionals. The volumes are designed for use as supplementary materials or as components in larger "homemade" anthologies, in both introductory and advanced courses, and for use as basic source materials for student research projects. They enable the teacher to expose students to current philosophy without the usual struggle over library copies of journals. In addition, these anthologies will be useful to scholars in fields bordering on philosophy—for example, law, linguistics, literature, mathematics, physics, psychology, and theology—who wish to find in convenient capsule form the best of recent philosophical thinking on subjects of interest to them. For readers in general, the series provides an opportunity to sample the actual substance and methods of contemporary philosophy.

JOEL FEINBERG
Princeton University

WESLEY C. SALMON
Indiana University

CONTENTS

vii

CREATIVITY IN THE ARTS

INTRODUCTION

VINCENT TOMAS

One of the notable features of our twentieth-century attitude toward art is the extraordinary veneration, amounting even to a cult, so many of us have for creativity.

If this needs to be shown, it is almost enough to allude to Pablo Picasso, whose immense reputation rests largely on the fact that he is regarded as a creative artist—as one who, throughout his long career, has been a restless inventor of forms and styles so fecund as to be dazzling.

But consider, too, that for most contemporary critics, collectors, and connoisseurs, a necessary condition for greatness in an artist is that he be creative. Consider how much of the research of art historians (it makes no difference whether the art be painting, sculpture, music, literature, architecture, or some other) is devoted to finding out just who it was that created something that disciples then merely "imitated." And consider, finally, how different the art-world scene of the past fifty

1

years probably would have been if so much of the energy of artists had not been poured into trying to be creative (something praiseworthy) and to avoid being academic (which for us is usually a term of contempt) ; or if some of them had had more clearly in mind just what it means for an artist to be creative.

What *does* it mean? Perhaps better, what after reflection do we really want to mean when we say that a certain artist is creative, or that a certain painting, symphony, poem, building, or other work is a work of creative art?

This question is a philosophical question, distinct from other, non-philosophical questions, interesting though the latter may be, with which it is sometimes confused. When one asks it, one is not inquiring for historical information about the work habits of artists; nor for what are the personal or social conditions most conducive to creativity in the arts; nor for what is the psychological explanation (if any) of creativity. Rather, one is asking for a clarification or analysis of the *concept* of creativity as applied to art. One wants to know explicitly the nature of artistic creation—to be given a description of the conditions an activity must satisfy if it is to be an instance of artistic creation rather than of something else.

For example, when we judge that an artist is creative, do we mean *merely* that he produces something different from what has been produced before—something that, when it is viewed against the background of the familiar and the traditional in art, is seen to be in some striking respect novel? For most of us, creativity certainly does imply novelty. But, if it implied nothing more, it would not differ in kind from blind experimentation and from what Bernard Berenson referred to as the "originality of incompetence"; and we would then be at a loss to account for the honorific overtones of the word "creative."

Anyone acquainted with the literature of art criticism will know that the sentence (1) "Jones is a creative artist" is sometimes used to formulate a judgment that might just as well have been formulated by (2) "Well, you have to grant that the things Jones produces are *different.*" From (2) it does not follow either that (3) "The things Jones produces are good" or (4) "Jones is deserving of praise for what he produces." Probably, for most of us, (3) and (4) *do* follow from (1). That is, we probably use (1) in such a way that if it is true, (3) and (4) must also be true. The point is that (3) and (4) would not follow from (1) if, for us, (1) "Jones is a creative artist" were identical in meaning to (2) "Well, you have to grant that the things Jones produces are *different*." There is nothing to prevent anyone from using (1) to mean (2), unless it be a desire for clarity and an unwillingness to bestow praise except where it is deserved.

For another example: Do we want to mean by creation in art *merely* the production of a work that not only is different but is different in a valuable way? In that case, it would follow that a computer would be no less creative than Beethoven was, if it produced a symphony as original and as great as one of his, or that a monkey conceivably could paint pictures which were no less works of creative art than Picasso's (indeed, it has been alleged that some monkeys have done so). So conceived, artistic creation is not necessarily an action, in the sense of this word that involves intention and critical control, and the traditional distinction between action and mere movement is obliterated. In three of the essays that follow, R. G. Collingwood, Eliseo Vivas, and C. J. Ducasse present arguments against such a view.

The essays that follow have been selected for the light, direct and indirect, they shed on the concept of creativity, and on its logical relations to other concepts. Those by Ben Shahn, Stephen Spender, and Wassily Kandinsky were written by artists at moments when they paused to reflect upon the nature and implications of their primary vocation. The others, except for the one by Bernard Berenson, are by philosophers. None of them is obscure, and I have nothing to say about them and their subject that is not already more or less said in the last essay. So it seems best to allow the authors to speak for themselves to their readers who are interested in clarifying their ideas about creativity in the arts.

MAKING AND CREATION

R. G. COLLINGWOOD

THE PROBLEM DEFINED

What is a work of art, granted that there is something in art proper (not only in art falsely so called) to which that name is applied, and that, since art is not craft, this thing is not an artifact? It is something made by the artist, but not made by transforming a given raw material, nor by carrying out a preconceived plan, nor by way of realizing the means to a preconceived end. What is this kind of making?

Here are two questions which, however closely they are connected, we shall do well to consider separately. We had better begin with the artist, and put the second question first. I shall therefore begin by asking: What is the nature of this making which is not technical making, or, if we want a one-word name for it, not fabrication? It is important not to misunderstand the question. When we asked what expres-

From The Principles of Art (*Oxford: The Clarendon Press, 1955*). *Reprinted by permission of The Clarendon Press.*

sion was, it was pointed out that the writer was not trying to construct an argument intended to convince the reader, not to offer him information, but to remind him of what (if he is a person whose experience of the subject-matter has been sufficient to qualify him for reading books of this kind) he knows already. So here. We are not asking for theories but for facts. And the facts for which we are asking are not recondite facts. They are facts well known to the reader. The order of facts to which they belong may be indicated by saying that they are the ways in which all of us who are concerned with art habitually think about it, and the ways in which we habitually express our thoughts in ordinary speech.

By way of making this clearer, I will indicate the kind of way in which our question cannot be answered. A great many people who have put to themselves the question "What is this making, characteristic of the artist, which is not a fabrication?" have sought an answer in some such way as the following: "This nontechnical making is plainly not an accidental making, for works of art could not be produced by accident.[1] Something must be in control. But if this is not the artist's skill, it cannot be his reason or will or consciousness. It must therefore be something else; either some controlling force outside the artist, in which case we may call it inspiration, or something inside him but other than his will and so forth. This must be either his body, in which case the production of a work of art is at bottom a physiological activity, or else it is something mental but unconscious, in which case the productive force is the artist's unconscious mind."

Many imposing theories of art have been built on these foundations. The first alternative, that the artist's activity is controlled by some divine or at least spiritual being that uses him as its mouthpiece, is out of fashion today, but that is no reason why we should refuse it a hearing. It does at least fit the facts better than most of the theories of

---

[1] I am talking of quite sensible people. There are others; some of them have denied this proposition, pointing out that if a monkey played with a typewriter for long enough, rattling the keys at random, there is a calculable probability that within a certain time he would produce, purely by accident, the complete text of Shakespeare. Any reader who has nothing to do can amuse himself by calculating how long it would take for the probability to be worth betting on. But the interest of the suggestion lies in the revelation of the mental state of a person who can identify the "works" of Shakespeare with the series of letters printed on the pages of a book bearing that phrase as its title; and thinks, if he can be said to think at all, that an archaeologist of 10,000 years hence, recovering a complete text of Shakespeare from the sands of Egypt but unable to read a single word of English, would possess Shakespeare's dramatic and poetic works.

art nowadays current. The second alternative, that the artist's work is controlled by forces which, though part of himself and specifically part of his mind, are not voluntary and not conscious, but work in some mental cellar unseen and unbidden by the dwellers in the house above, is extremely popular; not among artists, but among psychologists and their numerous disciples, who handle the theory with a great deal of confidence and seem to believe that by its means the riddle of art has at last been solved.[2] The third alternative was popular with the physiological psychologists of the last century, and Grant Allen still remains its best exponent.

It would be waste of time to criticize these theories. The question about them is not whether they are good or bad, considered as examples of theorizing; but whether the problem which they are meant to solve is one that calls for theorizing in order to solve it. A person who cannot find his spectacles on the table may invent any number of theories to account for their absence. They may have been spirited away by a benevolent deity, to prevent him from overworking, or by a malicious demon, to interfere with his studies, or by a neighboring mahatma, to convince him that such things can be done. He may have unconsciously made away with them himself, because they unconsciously remind him of his oculist, who unconsciously reminds him of his father, whom he unconsciously hates. Or he may have pushed them off the table while moving a book. But these theories, however ingenious and sublime, are premature if the spectacles should happen to be on his nose.

Theories professing to explain how works of art are constructed by means of hypotheses like these are based on recollecting that the spectacles are not on the table, and overlooking the fact that they are on the nose. Those who put them forward have not troubled to ask themselves whether we are in point of fact familiar with a kind of activity productive of results and under the agent's voluntary control, which has none of the special characteristics of craft. If they had asked the question, they must have answered it in the affirmative. We are perfectly familiar with activities of this kind; and our ordinary name for them is creation.

---

[2] Mr. Robert Graves [*Poetic Unreason* (London: Cecil Palmer, 1925)] is almost the only practicing man of letters or artist in this country who has come forward to back up the psychologists. Generally speaking, the judgment of literary men on the qualifications of the people who advocate this theory is sufficiently represented by Dr. I. A. Richards: "To judge by the published work of Freud upon Leonardo da Vinci or of Jung upon Goethe [e.g., *The Psychology of the Unconscious* (New York: Moffat, Yard & Co., 1916), p. 305] psychoanalysts tend to be peculiarly inept as critics" [*Principles of Literary Criticism* (London: Routledge & Kegan Paul, Ltd., 1934), pp. 29f.].

MAKING AND CREATING

Before we ask what in general are the occasions on which we use this word, we must forestall a too probable objection to the word itself. Readers suffering from theophobia will certainly by now have taken offense. Knowing as they do that theologians use it for describing the relation of God to the world, victims of this disease smell incense whenever they hear it spoken, and think it a point of honor that it shall never sully their lips or ears. They will by now have on the tips of their tongues all the familiar protests against an aesthetic mysticism that raises the function of art to the level of something divine and identifies the artist with God. Perhaps some day, with an eye on the Athanasian Creed, they will pluck up courage to excommunicate an arithmetician who uses the word three. Meanwhile, readers willing to understand words instead of shying at them will recollect that the word "create" is daily used in contexts that offer no valid ground for a fit of *odium theologicum*. If a witness in court says that a drunken man was creating a noise, or that a dance club has created a nuisance, if a historian says that somebody or other created the English navy or the Fascist state, if a publicist says that secret diplomacy creates international distrust, or the chairman of a company says that increased attention to advertisement will create an increased demand for its produce, no one expects a little man at the back of the room to jump up and threaten to leave unless the word is withdrawn. If he did, the stewards would throw him out for creating a disturbance.

To create something means to make it nontechnically, but yet consciously and voluntarily. Originally, *creare* means to generate, or make offspring, for which we still use its compound "procreate," and the Spaniards have *criatura,* for a child. The act of procreation is a voluntary act, and those who do it are responsible for what they are doing; but it is not done by any specialized form of skill. It need not be done (as it may be in the case of a royal marriage) as a means to any preconceived end. It need not be done (as it was by Mr. Shandy senior) according to any preconceived plan. It cannot be done (whatever Aristotle may say) by imposing a new form on any pre-existing matter. It is in this sense that we speak of creating a disturbance or a demand or a political system. The person who makes these things is acting voluntarily; he is acting responsibly; but he need not be acting in order to achieve any ulterior end; he need not be following a preconceived plan;

and he is certainly not transforming anything that can properly be called a raw material. It is in the same sense that Christians asserted, and neo-Platonists denied, that God created the world.

This being the established meaning of the word, it should be clear that when we speak of an artist as making a poem, or a play, or a painting, or a piece of music, the kind of making to which we refer is the kind we call creating. For, as we already know, these things, in so far as they are works of art proper, are not made as means to an end; they are not made according to any preconceived plan; and they are not made by imposing a new form upon a given matter. Yet they are made deliberately and responsibly, by people who know what they are doing, even though they do not know in advance what is going to come of it.

The creation which theologians ascribe to God is peculiar in one way and only one. The peculiarity of the act by which God is said to create the world is sometimes supposed to lie in this, that God is said to create the world "out of nothing," that is to say, without there being previously any matter upon which he imposes a new form. But that is a confusion of thought. In that sense, all creation is creation out of nothing. The peculiarity which is really ascribed to God is that in the case of his act there lacks not only a prerequisite in the shape of a matter to be transformed, but any prerequisite of any kind whatsoever. This would not apply to the creation of a child, or a nuisance, or a work of art. In order that a child should be created, there must be a whole world of organic and inorganic matter, not because the parents fabricate the child out of this matter, but because a child can come into existence, as indeed its parents can exist, only in such a world. In order that a nuisance should be created, there must be persons capable of being annoyed, and the person who creates the nuisance must already be acting in a manner which, if modified this way or that, would annoy them. In order that a work of art should be created, the prospective artist must have in him certain unexpressed emotions, and must also have the wherewithal to express them. In these cases, where creation is done by finite beings, it is obvious that these beings, because finite, must first be in circumstances that enable them to create. Because God is conceived as an infinite being, the creation ascribed to him is conceived as requiring no such conditions.

Hence, when I speak of the artist's relation to his works of art as that of a creator, I am not giving any excuse to unintelligent persons who think, whether in praise or dispraise of my notions, that I am raising the function of art to the level of something divine or making the artist into a kind of god.

CREATION AND IMAGINATION

We must proceed to a further distinction. All the things taken above as examples of things created are what we ordinarily call real things. A work of art need not be what we should call a real thing. It may be what we call an imaginary thing. A disturbance, or a nuisance, or a navy, or the like, is not created at all until it is created as a thing having its place in the real world. But a work of art may be completely created when it has been created as a thing whose only place is in the artist's mind.

Here, I am afraid, it is the metaphysician who will take offense. He will remind me that the distinction between real things and things that exist only in our minds is one to which he and his fellows have given a great deal of attention. They have thought about it so long and so intently that it has lost all meaning. Some of them have decided that the things we call real are only in our minds; others that the things we describe as being in our minds are thereby implied to be just as real as anything else. These two sects, it appears, are engaged in a truceless war, and any one who butts in by using the words about which they are fighting will be set upon by both sides and torn to pieces.

I do not hope to placate these gentlemen. I can only cheer myself up by reflecting that even if I go on with what I was saying they cannot eat me. If an engineer has decided how to build a bridge, but has not made any drawings or specifications for it on paper, and has not discussed his plan with anyone or taken any steps towards carrying it out, we are in the habit of saying that the bridge exists only in his mind, or (as we also say) in his head. When the bridge is built, we say that it exists not only in his head but in the real world. A bridge which "exists only in the engineer's head" we also call an imaginary bridge; one which "exists in the real world" we call a real bridge.

This may be a silly way of speaking; or it may be an unkind way of speaking, because of the agony it gives to metaphysicians; but it is a way in which ordinary people do speak, and ordinary people who speak in that way know quite well what kind of things they are referring to. The metaphysicians are right in thinking that difficult problems arise from talking in that way. Meanwhile, I shall go on "speaking with the vulgar"; if metaphysicians do not like it they need not read it.

The same distinction applies to such things as music. If a man has made up a tune but has not written it down or sung it or played it or done anything which could make it public property, we say that the tune exists only in his mind, or only in his head, or is an imaginary tune. If he sings or plays it, thus making a series of audible noises, we call this series of noises a real tune as distinct from an imaginary one.

When we speak of making an artifact we mean making a real artifact. If an engineer said that he had made a bridge, and when questioned turned out to mean that he had only made it in his head, we should think him a liar or a fool. We should say that he had not made a bridge at all, but only a plan for one. If he said he had made a plan for a bridge and it turned out that he had put nothing on paper, we should not necessarily think he had deceived us. A plan is a kind of thing that can only exist in a person's mind. As a rule, an engineer making a plan in his mind is at the same time making notes and sketches on paper; but the plan does not consist of what we call the "plans," that is, the pieces of paper with these notes and sketches on them. Even if he has put complete specifications and working drawings on paper, the paper with these specifications and drawings on it is not the plan; it only serves to tell people (including himself, for memory is fallible) what the plan is. If the specifications and drawings are published, for example in a treatise on civil engineering, any one who reads the treatise intelligently will get the plan of that bridge into his head. The plan is therefore public property, although by calling it public we mean only that it can get into the heads of many people; as many as read intelligently the book in which the specifications and drawings are published.

In the case of the bridge there is a further stage. The plan may be "executed" or carried out; that is to say, the bridge may be built. When that is done, the plan is said to be "embodied" in the built bridge. It has begun to exist in a new way, not merely in people's heads but in stone or concrete. From being a mere plan existing in people's heads, it has become the form imposed on certain matter. Looking back from that point of view, we can now say that the engineer's plan was the form of the bridge without its matter, or that when we describe him as having the plan in his mind we might equally have described him as having in mind the form of the finished bridge without its matter.

The making of the bridge is the imposing of this form on this matter. When we speak of the engineer as making the plan, we are using the work "make" in its other sense, as equivalent to create. Making a plan for a bridge is not imposing a certain form on a certain matter; it is a making that is not a transforming, that is to say, it is a creation. It has the other characteristics, too, that distinguish creating from fabricating. It need not be done as means to an end, for a man can make plans (for example, to illustrate a textbook of engineering) with no intention of executing them. In such a case the making of the plan is not means to composing the textbook, it is part of composing the textbook. It is not means to anything. Again, a person making a plan need not be carrying out a plan to make that plan. He may be doing this; he may for instance have planned a textbook for which he needs an example of a reinforced concrete bridge with a single span of 150 feet, to carry a two-track railway with a roadway above it, and he may work out a plan for such a bridge in order that it may occupy that place in the book. But this is not a necessary condition of planning. People sometimes speak as if everybody had, or ought to have, a plan for his whole life, to which every other plan he makes is or ought to be subordinated; but no one can do that.

Making an artifact, or acting according to craft, thus consists of two stages: (1) Making the plan, which is creating. (2) Imposing that plan on certain matter, which is fabricating. Let us now consider a case of creating where what is created is not a work of art. A person creating a disturbance need not be, though of course he may be, acting on a plan. He need not be, though of course he may be, creating it as means to some ulterior end, such as causing a government to resign. He cannot be transforming a pre-existing material, for there is nothing out of which a disturbance can be made; though he is able to create it only because he already stands, as a finite being always does stand, in a determinate situation; for example, at a political meeting. But what he creates cannot be something that exists only in his own mind. A disturbance is something in the minds of the people disturbed.

Next, let us take the case of a work of art. When a man makes up a tune, he may and very often does at the same time hum it or sing it or play it on an instrument. He may do none of these things, but write it on paper. Or he may both hum it or the like, and also write it on paper at the same time or afterwards. Also he may do these things in public, so that the tune at its very birth becomes public property, like the disturbance we have just considered. But all these are accessories of the real work, though some of them are very likely useful accessories. The actual making of the tune is something that goes on in his head, and nowhere else.

I have already said that a thing which "exists in a person's head" and nowhere else is alternatively called an imaginary thing. The actual making of the tune is therefore alternatively called the making of an imaginary tune. This is a case of creation, just as much as the making of a plan or a disturbance, and for the same reasons, which it would be tedious to repeat. Hence the making of a tune is an instance of imaginative creation. The same applies to the making of a poem, or a picture, or any other work of art.

The engineer, as we saw, when he made his plan in his own head, may proceed to do something else which we call "making his plans." His "plans," here, are drawings and specifications on paper, and these are artifacts made to serve a certain purpose, namely to inform others or remind himself of the plan. The making of them is accordingly not imaginative creation; indeed, it is not creation at all. It is fabrication, and the ability to do it is a specialized form of skill, the craft of engineer's draughtsmanship.

The artist, when he has made his tune, may go on to do something else which at first sight seems to resemble this: he may do what is called publishing it. He may sing or play it aloud, or write it down, and thus make it possible for others to get into their heads the same thing which he has in his. But what is written or printed on music-paper is not the tune. It is only something which when studied intelligently will enable others (or himself, when he has forgotten it) to construct the tune for themselves in their own heads.

The relation between making the tune in his head and putting it down on paper is thus quite different from the relation, in the case of the engineer, between making a plan for a bridge and executing that plan. The engineer's plan is embodied in the bridge: it is essentially a form that can be imposed on certain matter, and when the bridge is built the form is there, in the bridge, as the way in which the matter composing it is arranged. But the musician's tune is not there on the paper at all. What is on the paper is not music, it is only musical notation. The relation of the tune to the notation is not like the relation of the plan to the bridge; it is like the relation of the plan to the specifications and drawings; for these, too, do not embody the plan as the bridge embodies it, they are only a notation from which the abstract or as yet unembodied plan can be reconstructed in the mind of a person who studies them.

THE BIOGRAPHY

OF A PAINTING

BEN SHAHN

In 1948, while Henry McBride was still writing for the *New York Sun,* I exhibited a painting to which I had given the somewhat cryptic title, "Allegory." The central image of the painting was one which I had been developing across a span of months—a huge Chimera-like beast, its head wreathed in flames, its body arched across the figures of four recumbent children. These latter were dressed in very commonplace clothes, perhaps not entirely contemporary, but rather as I could draw them and their details from my own memory.

I had always counted Henry McBride as a friend and an admirer of my pictures, about which he had written many kind words. Even of this one, he wrote glowingly at first. Then he launched into a strange and angry analysis of the work, attributing to it political motives, suggesting

From The Shape of Content (*Cambridge, Mass.: Harvard University Press. Copyright, 1957, by the President and Fellows of Harvard College*). *Reprinted by permission of the author and Harvard University Press.*

some symbolism of Red Moscow, drawing parallels which I cannot recall accurately, but only their tone of violence, completing his essay by recommending that I, along with the Red Dean of Canterbury, be deported.

Mr. McBride's review was not the first astonishing piece of analysis of my work that I have read, nor was it the last. Perhaps, coming as it did from a critic whom I had looked upon as a friend, it was one of the most disconcerting. In any case, it caused me to undertake a review of this painting, "Allegory," to try to assess just for my own enlightenment what really was in it, what sort of things go to make up a painting. Of the immediate sources I was fully aware, but I wondered to what extent I could trace the deeper origins, and the less conscious motivations.

I had an additional reason for undertaking such an exploration besides the pique which Mr. McBride's review had engendered. I had long carried in my mind that famous critical credo of Clive Bell's, a credo which might well have been erased by time, but which instead has grown to almost tidal proportions and which still constitutes the Procrustean bed into which all art must be either stretched or shrunk. The credo runs as follows: "The representative element in a work of art may or may not be harmful, but it is always irrelevant. For to appreciate a work of art, we must bring with us nothing from life, no knowledge of its affairs and ideas, no familiarity with its emotions."

Once proffered as an isolated opinion, that view of art has now become a very dominant one, is taught in the schools, and is laboriously explained in the magazines. Thus, in reconsidering the elements which I feel have formed the painting "Allegory," I have had in mind both critical views, the one which presumes a symbolism beyond or aside from the intention of a painting, and the other, that which voids the work of art of any meaning, any emotion, or any intention.

The immediate source of the painting of the red beast was a Chicago fire in which a colored man had lost his four children. John Bartlow Martin had written a concise reportorial account of the event—one of those stories which, told in detail, without any emotionalism being present in the writing itself, manages to produce a far greater emotional impact than would a highly colored account.

I was asked to make drawings for the story and, after several discussions with the writer, felt that I had gained enough of the feel of the situation to proceed. I examined a great deal of factual visual material, and then I discarded all of it. It seemed to me that the implications of

this event transcended the immediate story; there was a universality about man's dread of fire, and his sufferings from fire. There was a universality in the pity which such a disaster invokes. Even racial injustice, which had played its part in this event, had its overtones. And the relentless poverty which had pursued this man, and which dominated the story, had its own kind of universality.

I now began to devise symbols of an almost abstract nature, to work in terms of such symbols. Then I rejected that approach too. For in the abstracting of an idea one may lose the very intimate humanity of it, and this deep and common tragedy was above all things human. I returned then to the small family contacts, to the familiar experiences of all of us, to the furniture, the clothes, the look of ordinary people, and on that level made my bid for universality and for the compassion that I hoped and believed the narrative would arouse.

Of all the symbols which I had begun or sought to develop, I retained only one in my illustrations—a highly formalized wreath of flames with which I crowned the plain shape of the house which had burned.

Sometimes, if one is particularly satisfied with a piece of work which he has completed, he may say to himself, "well done," and go on to

something else. Not in this instance, however. I found that I could not
dismiss the event about which I had made drawings—the so-called
"Hickman Story." In the first place, there were the half-realized, the
only intimated drawings in a symbolic direction which were lying
around my studio; I would develop some of them a little further to see
what might come of them. In the second place there was the fire itself;
I had some curious sense of responsibility about it, a sort of personal
involvement. I had still not fully expressed my sense of the enormity of
the Hickman fire; I had not formulated it in its full proportions; perhaps it was that I felt that I owed something more to the victim himself.

One cannot, I think, crowd into drawings a really towering content

of feeling. Drawings may be small intimate revelations; they may be witty or biting, they may be fragmentary glimpses of great feeling or awesome situation, but I feel that the immense idea asks for a full orchestration of color, depth, texture, and form.

The narrative of the fire had aroused in me a chain of personal memories. There were two great fires in my own childhood, one only colorful, the other disastrous and unforgettable. Of the first, I remember only that the little Russian village in which my grandfather lived burned, and I was there. I remember the excitement, the flames breaking out everywhere, the lines of men passing buckets to and from the river which ran through the town, the madwoman who had escaped from someone's house during the confusion, and whose face I saw, dead-white in all the reflected color.

The other fire left its mark upon me and all my family, and left its scars on my father's hands and face, for he had clambered up a drain-pipe and taken each of my brothers and sisters and me out of the house one by one, burning himself painfully in the process. Meanwhile our house and all our belongings were consumed, and my parents stricken beyond their power to recover.

Among my discarded symbols pertaining to the Hickman story there were a number of heads and bodies of beasts, besides several Harpies, Furies, and other symbolic, semi-classic shapes and figures. Of one of these, a lionlike head, but still not a lion, I made many drawings, each drawing approaching more nearly some inner figure of primitive terror which I was seeking to capture. I was beginning to become most familiar with this beast-head. It was, you might say, under control.

Of the other symbols I developed into paintings a good menagerie of Harpies, of birds with human heads, of curious and indecipherable beasts all of which I enjoyed immensely, and each of which held just enough human association for me to be great fun, and held just enough classical allusion to add a touch of elegance which I also enjoyed. (And this group of paintings in turn led off into a series of paintings of more or less classical allusion, some only pleasant, but some which like the "City of Dreadful Night" or "Momeric Struggle" were major paintings to me, each having, beside its classical allusion, a great deal of additional motivation.)

When I at last turned the lionlike beast into a painting, I felt able to imbue it with everything that I had ever felt about a fire. I incorporated the highly formalized flames from the Hickman story as a

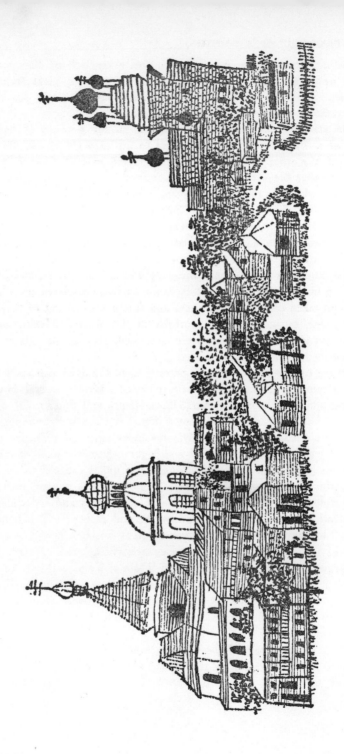

terrible wreath about its head, and under its body I placed the four child figures which, to me, hold the sense of all the helpless and the innocent.

The image that I sought to create was not one of *a* disaster; that somehow doesn't interest me. I wanted instead to create the emotional tone that surrounds disaster; you might call it the inner disaster.

In the beast as I worked upon it I recognized a number of creatures; there was something of the stare of an abnormal cat that we once owned that had devoured its own young. And then, there was the wolf.

To me, the wolf is perhaps the most paralyzingly dreadful of beasts, whether symbolic or real. Is my fear some instinctive strain out of my Russian background? I don't know. Is it merely the product of some of my mother's colorful tales about being pursued by wolves when she was with a wedding party, or again when she went alone from her village to another one nearby? Does it come from reading Gogol? Whatever its source, my sense of panic concerning the wolf is real. I sought to implant, or, better, I recognized something of that sense within my allegorical beast.

Then, to go on with the wolf image: I had always found disconcerting the familiar sculpture of Romulus and Remus being suckled by the She-Wolf. It had irritated me immensely, and was a symbol that I

abhorred. Now I found that, whether by coincidence or not I am unable
to say, the stance of my imaginary beast was just that of the great
Roman wolf, and that the children under its belly might almost be a
realization of my vague fears that, instead of suckling the children, the
wolf would most certainly destroy them. But the children, in their
play-clothes of 1908, are not Roman, nor are they the children of the
Hickman fire; they resemble much more closely my own brothers and
sisters.

Such are a few of the traceable sources of imagery, and of the feeling
of a single painting—mine, only because I can know what these sources
are, because I am able to follow them backward at least to that point
at which they disappear into the limbo of the subconscious, or the
unconscious, or the instinctive, or the merely biological.

But there are many additional components present within a painting, many other factors that modify, impel, restrain, and in unison
shape the images which finally emerge.

The restraining factors alone wield a powerful, albeit only negative,
invisible hand. An artist at work upon a painting must be two people,
not one. He must function and act as two people all the time and in
several ways. On the one hand, the artist is the imaginer and the pro-
ducer. But he is also the critic, and here is a critic of such inexorable
standards as to have made McBride seem liberal even in his most
illiberal moment.

When a painting is merely in the visionary stage, the inner critic
has already begun stamping upon it. The artist is enthusiastic about
some idea that he has. "You cannot," says the inner critic, "superimpose
upon visual material that which is not essentially visual. Your idea is
underdeveloped. You must find an image in which the feeling itself is
embedded. An image of a fire? Not at all! A fire is a cheerful affair. It
is full of bright colors and moving shapes; it makes everybody happy.
It is not your purpose to tell about a fire, not to describe a fire. Not at
all; what you want to formulate is the terror, the heart-shaking fear.
Now, find that image!"

So the inward critic has stopped the painting before it has even been
begun. Then, when the artist strips his idea down to emotional images
alone and begins slowly, falteringly, moving toward some realization,
that critic is constantly objecting, constantly chiding, holding the hand
back to the image alone, so that the painting remains only that, so that
it does not split into two things, one, the image, and another, the
meaning.

I have never met a literary critic of painting who, whatever his sentiments toward the artist, would actually destroy an existing painting. He would regard such an act as vandalism and would never consider it. But the critic within the artist is a ruthless destroyer. He continually rejects the contradictory elements within a painting, the colors that do not act upon other colors and would thus constitute dead places within his work; he rejects insufficient drawing; he rejects forms and colors incompatible with the intention or mood of the piece; he rejects intention itself and mood itself often as banal or derivative. He mightily applauds the good piece of work; he cheers the successful passage; but then if the painting does not come up to his standards he casts aside everything and obliterates the whole.

The critic within the artist is prompted by taste, highly personal, experienced and exacting. He will not tolerate within a painting any element which strays very far from that taste.

During the early French-influenced part of my artistic career, I painted landscapes in a Post-Impressionist vein, pleasantly peopled with bathers, or I painted nudes, or studies of my friends. The work had a nice professional look about it, and it rested, I think, on a fairly solid academic training. It was during those years that the inner critic first began to play hara-kiri with my insides. With such ironic words as, "It has a nice professional look about it," my inward demon was prone to ridicule or tear down my work in just those terms in which I was wont to admire it.

The questions, "Is that enough? Is that all?" began to plague me. Or, "This may be art, but is it my own art?" And then I began to realize that however professional my work might appear, even however original it might be, it still did not contain the central person which, for good or ill, was myself. The whole stream of events and of thinking and changing thinking; the childhood influences that were still strong in me; my rigorous training as a lithographer with its emphasis upon craft; my several college years with the strong intention to become a biologist; summers at Woods Hole, the probing of the wonders of marine forms; all my views and notions on life and politics, all this material and much more which must constitute the substance of whatever person I was, lay outside the scope of my own painting. Yes, it was art that I was producing, perfectly competent, but foreign to me, and the inner critic was rising up against it.

It was thus under the pressure of such inner rejection that I first began to ask myself what sort of person I really was, and what kind of art could truly coincide with that person. And to bring into this question the matter of taste I felt—or the inner critic felt—that it was both tawdry and trivial to wear the airs and the artistic dress of a society to which I did not belong.

I feel, I even know, that this first step in rejection is a presence within the fire-image painting of which I have undertaken to speak. The moving toward one's inner self is a long pilgrimage for a painter. It offers many temporary successes and high points, but there is always the residuum of incomplete realization which impels him on toward the more adequate image.

Thus there began for me the long artistic tug of war between idea and image.

At first, the danger of such a separation did not appear. For my first disquisition in paint was only semi-serious. My friend Walker Evans and I had decided to set up an exhibition in the barn of a Portuguese family on Cape Cod. He would exhibit a series of superb photographs which he had made of the family there; I would exhibit a few water colors, most of them not yet in existence.

At just that time I was absorbed in a small book which I had picked up in France, a history of the Dreyfus case. I would do some exposition of the affair in pictures. So I set to work and presented the leading malefactors of the case, the defenders, and of course Dreyfus himself. Under each portrait I lettered in my best lithographic script a long or short legend setting forth the role which the original of the portrait had played in the celebrated affair.

What had been undertaken lightly became very significant in my eyes. Within the Dreyfus pictures I could see a new avenue of expression opening up before me, a means by which I could unfold a great deal of my most personal thinking and feeling without loss of simplicity. I felt that the very directness of statement of these pictures was a great virtue in itself. And I further felt, and perhaps hoped a little, that such simplicity would prove irritating to that artistic elite who had already— even at the end of the twenties—begun to hold forth "disengagement" as the first law of creation. As artists of a decade or so earlier had delighted to *épater le bourgeois,* so I found it pleasant, to borrow a line from Leonard Baskin, to *épater l'avant-garde.*

Having returned only recently from France where the Sacco-Vanzetti case was a national fever, I now turned to that noted drama for the theme of a new group of paintings, and set about revealing the acts and the persons involved with as rigorous a simplicity as I could command.

I was not unmindful of Giotto, and of the simplicity with which he had been able to treat of connected events—each complete in itself, yet all recreating the religious drama, so living a thing to him.

The ensuing series of pictures was highly rewarding to me. First, I felt that my own work was now becoming identified with my person. Then there was the kind of response which met the pictures; not only did the customary art public receive the work kindly, but there was also an entirely new kind of public, a great influx of people who do not ordinarily visit galleries—journalists and Italian immigrants and many other sorts of sympathizers. And then there was the book about the case which Benchley sent to me, inscribed, "to Ben Shahn without whom this crime could never have been committed."

I continued to work in terms of pictures which related to a central theme, the inner critic being somewhat appeased and exercising only a certain technical stringency. A new series of questions now arose for me, and with them the inevitable consequent rejections. I began to question the degree of my belief in the views which I held. It became uncomfortably apparent to me that whatever one thinks as well as whatever one paints must be constantly re-examined, torn apart, if that seems to be indicated, and reassembled in the light of new attitudes or new discovery. If one has set for himself the position that his painting shall not misconstrue his personal mode of thinking, then he must be rather unusually alert to just what he does think.

I was impelled to question the social view of man to which I had adhered for a number of years without actually doubting that it might be either a right view or a natural one to me. Now it dawned upon me that I had always been at war with this idea. Generalities and abstractions and vital statistics had always bored me. Whether in people or in art it was the individual peculiarities that were interesting. One has sympathy with a hurt person, not because he is a generality, but precisely because he is not. Only the individual can imagine, invent, or create. The whole audience of art is an audience of individuals. Each of them comes to the painting or sculpture because there he can be told that he, the individual, transcends all classes and flouts all predictions. In the work of art he finds his uniqueness affirmed.

Yes, one rankles at broad injustices, and one ardently hopes for and works toward mass improvements; but that is only because whatever mass there may be is made up of individuals, and each of them is able to feel and have hopes and dreams.

Nor would such a view invalidate a belief which I had held about the unifying power of art. I have always believed that the character of a society is largely shaped and unified by its great creative works, that a society is molded upon its epics, and that it imagines in terms of its created things—its cathedrals, its works of art, its musical treasures, its literary and philosophic works. One might say that a public may be so unified because the highly personal experience is held in common by the many individual members of the public. The great moment at which Oedipus in his remorse tears out his eyes is a private moment—one of deepest inward emotion. And yet that emotion, produced by art, and many other such private and profound emotions, experiences, and images bound together the Greek people into a great civilization, and bound others all over the earth to them for all time to come.

So I had crossed the terrain of the "social view," and I would not return. At the same time, I feel that all such artistic terrain which one has crossed must to some extent affect or modify his later work. Whatever one has rejected is in itself a tangible shaping force. That all such work improves the skill of the hand or the discernment of the eye is only a minor consideration. Even of one's thinking, however much his views may change, one retains a great deal, rejecting only that which seems foreign to him or irrelevant. Or, one may wholly reject the social view of man and at the same time cherish its underlying sympathies and its sense of altruism.

Such a process of acceptance and rejection—the artist plus the inner critic—or you might just say, the informed creator—is present in the most fragmentary piece which an artist produces. A small sketch of Picasso's, a drawing by Rouault, or Manet or Modigliani, is not to be dismissed as negligible, for any such piece contains inevitably the long evolutionary process of taste, deftness, and personal view. It is, if brief, still dictated by the same broad experience and personal understanding which molds the larger work.

I was not the only artist who had been entranced by the social dream, and who could no longer reconcile that view with the private and inner objectives of art. As during the thirties art had been swept by mass ideas, so during the forties there took place a mass movement toward abstraction. Not only was the social dream rejected, but any dream at all. Many of those names that, during the thirties, had been affixed to paintings of hypothetical tyrannies and theoretical cures were now affixed to cubes and cones and threads and swirls of paint. Part of that work was—and is—beautiful and meaningful; part of it does indeed constitute private experience. A great part of it also represents only the rejection, only the absence of self-commitment.

The change in art, mine included, was accomplished during World War II. For me, it had begun during the late thirties when I worked in the Resettlement Administration. I had then crossed and recrossed many sections of the country, and had come to know well so many people of all kinds of belief and temperament, which they maintained with a transcendent indifference to their lot in life. Theories had melted before such experience. My own painting then had turned from what is called "social realism" into a sort of personal realism. I found the qualities of people a constant pleasure; there was the coal miner, a cellist, who organized a quartet for me—the quartet having three musicians. There was the muralist who painted the entire end of his barn with scenes of war and then of plenty, the whole painting entitled "Uncle Sam Did It All." There were the five Musgrove brothers who played five harmonicas—the wonderful names of people, Plato Jordan and Jasper Lancaster, and of towns, Pity Me, and Tail Holt, and Bird-in-Hand. There were the poor who were rich in spirit, and the rich who were also sometimes rich in spirit. There was the South and its storytelling art, stories of snakes and storms and haunted houses, enchanting; and yet such talent thriving in the same human shell with hopeless prejudices, bigotry, and ignorance.

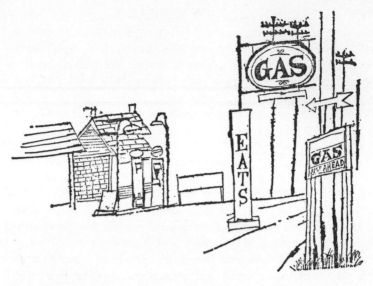

Personal realism, personal observation of the way of people, the mood of life and places; all that is a great pleasure, but I felt some larger potentiality in art.

During the war I worked in the Office of War Information. We were supplied with a constant stream of material, photographic and other kinds of documentation of the decimation within enemy territory. There were the secret confidential horrible facts of the cartloads of dead; Greece, India, Poland. There were the blurred pictures of bombed-out places, so many of which I knew well and cherished. There were the churches destroyed, the villages, the monasteries—Monte Cassino and Ravenna. At that time I painted only one theme, "Europa," you might call it. Particularly I painted Italy as I lamented it, or feared that it might have become.

It had been my principle in painting, during all the changes that I had undertaken, that outer objects or people must be observed with an acute eye for detail, but that all such observation must be molded from an inner view. I had felt consistently, also, that any such content must be painted in a way wholly subject to the kind of medium, whether oil, tempera, fresco, or whatever.

But now I saw art turning abstract, courting material alone. It seemed to me that such a direction promised only a cul-de-sac for the painter. I wanted to avoid that direction, and at the same time I wanted to find some deeper source of meaning in art, a constant spring that would not run dry with the next change in political weather.

Out of the battery of acceptances and rejections that mold the style of a painter, there rises as a force not only his own growing and changing work, but that of other work, both contemporary and past. He must observe all these directions and perhaps continue those which appear to be fruitful, while shunning those which appear to be limited and of short duration. Thus a degree of sophistication is essential to the painter.

While I felt a growing conviction as to the validity of the inner view, I wanted not to retread the ground which had been so admirably illuminated by Surrealism. Indeed the subconscious, the unconscious, the dream-world does offer a rich, almost limitless, panorama for the explorations of art; but in that approach, I think we may call it the psychological approach, one may discern beyond the rich imagery certain limits and inevitable pitfalls.

The limitation which circumscribed Surrealist art arose from its effort to reveal the subconscious. For in that effort control and intention were increasingly relinquished. Surrealism and the psychological approach

led into that quagmire of the so-called automatic practices of art—the biomorphic, the fecal, the natal, and the other absurdities.

The subconscious may greatly shape one's art; undoubtedly it does so. But the subconscious cannot create art. The very act of making a painting is an intending one; thus to intend and at the same time relinquish intention is a hopeless contradiction, albeit one that is exhibited on every hand.

But the great failure of all such art, at least in my own view, lies in the fact that man's most able self is his conscious self—his intending self. The psychological view can at best, even assuming that it were accurate, tell us what man is in spite of himself. It may perhaps discover those animal motives which are said to lurk beneath the human ones. It may unmask selfish purposes lying within altruism. It may even be able to reveal primitive psychological states underneath the claims and achievements of philosophy—the brute beneath the intellect. But the values of man, if he has any at all, reside in his intentions, in the degree to which he has moved away from the brute, in his intellect at its peak and in his humanity at its peak.

I do not conceive it to be the role of art to retrogress either into the prenatal or into the prehuman state. So while I accept the vast inner landscape that extends off the boundaries of consciousness to be almost infinitely fruitful of images and symbols, I know that such images mean one thing to the psychologist and quite another to the artist.

One might return to Oedipus. For, to the psychologist, Oedipus is a symbol of aberration only—a medical symbol. But to the artist Oedipus is a symbol of moral anguish, and even more than that, of transcendent spiritual power.

Or, consider Van Gogh; to the psychologist it is the periodic insanity of Van Gogh that is pre-eminent, and the psychologist deduces much from that. But to the artist it is clear that it was the great love of things and of people and the incredible suffering of Van Gogh that made his art possible and his insanity inevitable.

I know that there must be an ingredient of complete belief in any work of art—belief in what one is doing. I do not doubt that those artists who work only for pure form believe in form alone as the ultimate possible expression in art. Those who look upon their art as therapy probably believe with equal fervor in what they are doing. And I am sure that the artists who only manipulate materials believe firmly in that method. But here again one must be impelled by rejection. Such art can contain nothing of experience either inward or outward. It is only a painted curtain resting midway between the subjective and the objective, closing either off from the other.

To me both subjective and objective are of paramount importance, another aspect of the problem of image and idea. The challenge is not to abolish both from art, but rather to unite them into a single impression, an image of which meaning is an inalienable part.

I had once believed that the incidental, the individual, and the topical were enough; that in such instances of life all of life could be implied.

But then I came to feel that that was not enough. I wanted to reach farther, to tap some sort of universal experience, to create symbols that would have some such universal quality.

I made a series of paintings during the war which, in my own view —and what other view has an artist?—began to realize this more difficult objective. I shall discuss the pictures themselves, but again it is necessary to emphasize the conflict which arises in any such change of view, and the painful necessity to be aware of what one really thinks and wants in art.

I have already mentioned my personal dislike of generalities. Now, one must ask, is not the universal merely another term for the generality? How can one actually achieve a universality in painting without becoming merely more generalized and abstract? I feel that this question is one which greatly concerns artists. Its resolution will greatly affect the kind of an artist one is to be.

My own approach can only be to ask myself just why it is that I so dislike all statistics and most generalities. The answer that I find is simply that I dislike such material because it is impersonal. In being average to all things, it is particular to none. If we were to attempt to construct an "average American" we would necessarily put together an effigy which would have the common qualities of all Americans, but would have the eccentricities, peculiarities, and unique qualities of no American. It would, like the sociologist's statistical high-school student, approximate everyone and resemble no one.

But let us say that the universal is that unique thing which affirms the unique qualities of all things. The universal experience is that private experience which illuminates the private and personal world in which each of us lives the major part of his life. Thus, in art, the symbol which has vast universality may be some figure drawn from the most remote and inward recesses of consciousness; for it is here that we are unique and sovereign and most wholly aware. I think of Masaccio's "Expulsion from the Garden," so intensely personal that it leaves no

person untouched. I think of a di Chirico figure, lonely in a lonely street haunted by shadows; its loneliness speaks to all human loneliness. As an experience, neither painting has anything of the average; both come from extreme limits of feeling and both paintings have a great universality.

The paintings which I made toward the close of the war—the "Liberation" picture, "The Red Staircase," "Pacific Landscape," "Cherubs and Children," "Italian Landscape," and quite a number of others did not perhaps depart sharply in style or appearance from my earlier work, but they had become more private and more inward-looking. A symbolism which I might once have considered cryptic now became the only means by which I could formulate the sense of emptiness and waste that the war gave me, and the sense of the littleness of people trying to live on through the enormity of war. I think that at that time I was very little concerned with communication as a conscious objective. Formulation itself was enough of a problem—to formulate into images, into painted surfaces, feelings, which, if obscure, were at least strongly felt.

But in my own view these paintings were successful. I found in them a way to go, actually a liberation of sorts for myself. I became most conscious then that the emotional image is not necessarily of that event in the outside world which prompts our feeling; the emotional image is rather made up of the inner vestiges of many events. It is of that company of phantoms which we all own and which have no other sense than the fear sense, or that of the ludicrous, or of the terribly beautiful; images that have the nostalgia of childhood with possibly none of the facts of our childhood; images which may be drawn only from the recollection of paint upon a surface, and yet that have given one great exaltation—such are the images to be sensed and formulated.

I became increasingly preoccupied with the sense and the look, indeed, with the power of this newly emerging order of image. It was, as I have indicated, a product of active intentions plus the constant demands and rejections of the inward critic; even perhaps of a certain striving to measure my own work critically with some basic truth in art. At the same time I read and do read comments about my work by outer critics, some referring to the work as "Social Realism," some lamenting its degree of content, holding that to be irrelevant to any art, but most employing certain labels which, however friendly they may be in intention, have so little relation to the context of a painting. I believe that if it were left to artists to choose their own labels most would choose none. For most artists have expended a great deal of energy in scrambling out of classes and categories and pigeon-holes, aspiring toward some state of perfect freedom which unfortunately neither human limitations nor the law allows—not to mention the critics.

I don't just think, I know, that this long historical process which I have just described is present within the one painting of the fire animal which is called "Allegory." There is considerable content which extends through one's work, appearing, disappearing, changing, growing; there is the shaping power of rejection which I have discussed, and the constant activity of revising one's ideas—of thinking what one wants to think. All these elements are present to a greater or less degree in the work of any painter who is deeply occupied in trying to impress his personality upon inert matter.

But allowing all this procedure and material, I must now say that it is, in another sense, only background. It is formulative of taste; it is the stuff and make-up of the inner critic; it is the underground stream of ideas. But idea itself must always bow to the needs and demands of the material in which it is to be cast. The painter who stands before an empty canvas must think in terms of paint. If he is just beginning in the use of paint, the way may be extremely difficult for him because he may not yet have established a complete rapport with his medium. He does not yet know what it can do, and what it cannot do. He has not yet discovered that paint has a power by itself and in itself—or where that power lies, or how it relates to him. For with the practiced painter it is that relationship which counts; his inner images are paint images, as those of the poet are no doubt metrical word images and those of the musician tonal images.

From the moment at which a painter begins to strike figures of color upon a surface he must become acutely sensitive to the feel, the textures, the light, the relationships which arise before him. At one point he will mold the material according to an intention. At another he may yield intention—perhaps his whole concept—to emerging forms, to new implications within the painted surface. Idea itself—ideas, many ideas move back and forth across his mind as a constant traffic, dominated perhaps by larger currents and directions, by what he wants to think. Thus idea rises to the surface, grows, changes as a painting grows and develops. So one must say that painting is both creative and responsive. It is an initimately communicative affair between the painter and his painting, a conversation back and forth, the painting telling the painter even as it receives its shape and form.

Here too, the inward critic is ever at hand, perpetually advising and casting doubt. Here the work is overstated; there it is thin; in another place, muddiness is threatened; somewhere else it has lost connection with the whole; here it looks like an exercise in paint alone; there, an area should be preserved; thus the critic, sometimes staying the hand of the painter, sometimes demanding a fresh approach, sometimes demanding that a whole work be abandoned—and sometimes not succeeding, for the will may be stubborn enough to override such good advice.

I have spoken of the tug of war between idea and image which at an earlier time in my painting had plagued me so greatly. I could not reconcile that conflict by simply abandoning idea, as so many artists had done. Such an approach may indeed simplify painting, but it also removes it from the arena of challenging, adult, fully intellectual and mature practice. For me, there would be little reason for painting if idea were not to emerge from the work. I cannot look upon myself or upon man generally as a merely behaving species. If there is value it rests upon the human ability to have idea, and indeed upon the stature of the idea itself.

The painting of the Red Beast, "Allegory," is an idea painting. It is also a highly emotional painting, and I hope that it is still primarily an image, a paint image. I began the painting, as I have said, with no established idea, only with the sense of a debt to be paid and with a clamoring of images, many of them. But as to the fire itself, and as to fires, I had many ideas, a whole subcontinent of ideas, none of which would be executed to measure, but any one of which might rise to become the dominating force in the painting. So it was with the series of paintings which I made during and after the time of the fire animal. There was the painting "Brothers." Paint, yes, but also reunion, reconciliation, end of war, pain of strong feeling, family, brothers. There was the painting called "City of Dreadful Night"—a forest of television aerials—lines in paint—splashes of light, or heads of ancient demons tangled in the antennae—a somber building with moldering Greek heads. All of these images arose out of paint, yes, but they also arose out of the somewhat ominous implications of television for the mind, for the culture. Out of a chain of connective ideas, responding to paint and color, rises the image, the painted idea. Thus the work may turn in an amusing direction, in a satirical direction. Or sometimes images are found—image ideas which are capable of great amplification, which can be built up to a high point of expressive power, at least for my purposes.

I cannot question that such a two-way communication has always constituted the painting process, sometimes with greater insistence of idea, sometimes with less, or none. Personal style, be it that of Michelangelo, or that of Tintoretto, or of Titian or of Giotto, has always been that peculiar personal rapport which has developed between an artist and his medium.

So I feel that painting is by no means a limited medium, neither limited to idea alone, nor to paint alone. I feel that painting is able to contain whatever one thinks and all that he is. The images which may be drawn out of colored materials may have depth and luminosity measured by the artist's own power to recognize and respond to such qualities, and to develop them. Painting may reflect, even brilliantly, the very limitations of an artist, the innocence of eye of a Rousseau, of a Bombois, of a John Kane. Painting can, and it has at various times, contained the whole of scholarship. Painting can contain the politician in a Daumier, the insurgent in a Goya, the suppliant in a Masaccio. It is not a spoken idea alone, nor a legend, nor a simple use or intention that forms what I have called the biography of a painting. It is rather the wholeness of thinking and feeling within an individual; it is partly his time and place; it is partly his childhood or even his adult fears and pleasures, and it is very greatly his thinking what he wants to think. Wrote Rilke:

> For the sake of a few lines one must see many cities, men and things. One must know the animals, one must feel how the birds fly and know the gesture with which the small flowers open in the morning. One must be able to think back to roads in unknown regions, to unexpected meetings and to partings which one had long seen coming; to days of childhood that are still unexplained, to parents that one had to hurt when they brought one some joy and one did not grasp it (it was a joy for someone else); to childhood illness that so strangely began with a number of profound and grave transformations, to days in rooms withdrawn and quiet and to mornings by the sea, to the sea itself, to seas, to nights of travel that rushed along on high and flew with all the stars—and it is not yet enough if one may think all of this. One must have memories of many nights of love, none of which was like the others, of the screams of women in labor, and of light, white, sleeping women in childbed, closing again. But one must also have been beside the dying, one must have sat beside the dead in the room with the open window and the fitful noises. And still it is not enough to have memories. One must be able to forget them when they are many, and one must have the great patience to wait until they come again. For it is not yet the memories themselves. Not until they have turned to blood within us, to glance, to gesture, nameless and no longer to be distinguished from ourselves—not until then can it happen that in a most rare hour the first word of a verse arises in their midst and goes forth from them.[1]

---

[1] From *The Notebooks of Malte Laurids Brigge,* M. D. Herter Norton, trans. (New York: W. W. Norton & Company, Inc., 1949).

THE MAKING OF A POEM

STEPHEN SPENDER

CONCENTRATION

The problem of creative writing is essentially one of concentration, and the supposed eccentricities of poets are usually due to mechanical habits or rituals developed in order to concentrate. Concentration, of course, for the purposes of writing poetry, is different from the kind of concentration required for working out a sum. It is a focusing of the attention in a special way, so that the poet is aware of all the implications and possible developments of his idea, just as one might say that a plant was not concentrating on developing mechanically in one direction, but in many directions, towards the warmth and light with its leaves, and towards the water with its roots, all at the same time.

Schiller liked to have a smell of rotten apples, concealed beneath the

From Partisan Review, *Vol. XIII, No. 3 (1946). Reprinted by permission of* Partisan Review.

lid of his desk, under his nose when he was composing poetry. Walter
de la Mare has told me that he must smoke when writing. Auden
drinks endless cups of tea. Coffee is my own addiction, besides smoking
a great deal, which I hardly ever do except when I am writing. I
notice also that as I attain a greater concentration, this tends to make
me forget the taste of the cigarette in my mouth, and then I have a
desire to smoke two or even three cigarettes at a time, in order that the
sensation from the outside may penetrate through the wall of concentration which I have built round myself.

For goodness sake, though, do not think that rotten apples or cigarettes or tea have anything to do with the quality of the work of a
Schiller, a de la Mare, or an Auden. They are a part of a concentration
which has already been attained rather than the causes of concentration.
De la Mare once said to me that he thought the desire to smoke when
writing poetry arose from a need, not of a stimulus, but to canalize
a distracting leak of his attention away from his writing towards the
distraction which is always present in one's environment. Concentration
may be disturbed by someone whistling in the street or the ticking of a
clock. There is always a slight tendency of the body to sabotage the
attention of the mind by providing some distraction. If this need for
distraction can be directed into one channel—such as the odor of rotten
apples or the taste of tobacco or tea—then other distractions outside
oneself are put out of competition.

Another possible explanation is that the concentrated effort of writing
poetry is a spiritual activity which makes one completely forget, for
the time being, that one has a body. It is a disturbance of the balance
of body and mind and for this reason one needs a kind of anchor of
sensation with the physical world. Hence the craving for a scent or
taste or even, sometimes, for sexual activity. Poets speak of the necessity
of writing poetry rather than of a liking for doing it. It is spiritual
compulsion, a straining of the mind to attain heights surrounded by
abysses and it cannot be entirely happy, for in the most important sense,
the only reward worth having is absolutely denied: for, however con-
fident a poet may be, he is never quite sure that all his energy is not
misdirected nor that what he is writing is great poetry. At the moment
when art attains its highest attainment it reaches beyond its medium
of words or paints or music, and the artist finds himself realizing that
these instruments are inadequate to the spirit of what he is trying to say.

Different poets concentrate in different ways. In my own mind I
make a sharp distinction between two types of concentration: one is

immediate and complete, the other is plodding and only completed by stages. Some poets write immediately works which, when they are written, scarcely need revision. Others write their poems by stages, feeling their way from rough draft to rough draft, until finally, after many revisions, they have produced a result which may seem to have very little connection with their early sketches.

These two opposite processes are vividly illustrated in two examples drawn from music: Mozart and Beethoven. Mozart thought out symphonies, quartets, even scenes from operas, entirely in his head—often on a journey or perhaps while dealing with pressing problems—and then he transcribed them, in their completeness, onto paper. Beethoven wrote fragments of themes in notebooks which he kept beside him, working on and developing them over years. Often his first ideas were of a clumsiness which makes scholars marvel how he could, at the end, have developed from them such miraculous results.

Thus genius works in different ways to achieve its ends. But although the Mozartian type of genius is the more brilliant and dazzling, genius, unlike virtuosity, is judged by greatness of results, not by brilliance of performance. The result must be the fullest development in a created aesthetic form of an original moment of insight, and it does not matter whether genius devotes a lifetime to producing a small result if that result be immortal. The difference between two types of genius is that one type (the Mozartian) is able to plunge the greatest depths of his own experience by the tremendous effort of a moment, the other (the Beethovenian) must dig deeper and deeper into his consciousness, layer by layer. What counts in either case is the vision which sees and pursues and attains the end; the logic of the artistic purpose.

A poet may be divinely gifted with a lucid and intense and purposive intellect; he may be clumsy and slow; that does not matter, what matters is integrity of purpose and the ability to maintain the purpose without losing oneself. Myself, I am scarcely capable of immediate concentration in poetry. My mind is not clear, my will is weak, I suffer from an excess of ideas and a weak sense of form. For every poem that I begin to write, I think of at least ten which I do not write down at all. For every poem which I do write down, there are seven or eight which I never complete.

The method which I adopt therefore is to write down as many ideas as possible, in however rough a form, in notebooks (I have at least twenty of these, on a shelf beside my desk, going back over fifteen years). I then make use of some of the sketches and discard others.

The best way of explaining how I develop the rough ideas which I use, is to take an example. Here is a notebook begun in 1944. About a hundred pages of it are covered with writing, and from this have emerged about six poems. Each idea, when it first occurs is given a number. Sometimes the ideas do not get beyond one line. For example No. 3 (never developed) is the one line:

A language of flesh and roses.

I shall return to this line in a few pages, when I speak of inspiration. For the moment, I turn to No. 13, because here is an idea which has been developed to its conclusion. The first sketch begins thus:

a)   There are some days when the sea lies like a harp
     Stretched flat beneath the cliffs. The waves
     Like wires burn with the sun's copper glow
                [all the murmuring blue
                     every silent]

     Between whose spaces every image
     Of sky [field and] hedge and field and boat
     Dwells like the huge face of the afternoon.
     [Lies]

     When the heat grows tired, the afternoon
     Out of the land may breathe a sigh
     [Across these wires like a hand. They vibrate
     With]
     Which moves across those wires like a soft hand
     [Then the vibration]
     Between whose spaces the vibration holds
     Every bird-cry, dog's bark, man-shout
     And creak of rollock from the land and sky
     With all the music of the afternoon.

Obviously these lines are attempts to sketch out an idea which exists clearly enough on some level of the mind where it yet eludes the attempt to state it. At this stage, a poem is like a face which one seems to be able to visualize clearly in the eye of memory, but when one examines it mentally or tries to think it out, feature by feature, it seems to fade.

The idea of this poem is a vision of the sea. The faith of the poet is that if this vision is clearly stated it will be significant. The vision is of the sea stretched under a cliff. On top of the cliff there are fields, hedges, houses. Horses draw carts along lanes, dogs bark far inland, bells ring in the distance. The shore seems laden with hedges, roses, horses and men, all high above the sea, on a very fine summer day when the ocean seems to reflect and absorb the shore. Then the small strung-out glittering waves of the sea lying under the shore are like the strings of a harp which catch the sunlight. Between these strings lies the reflection of the shore. Butterflies are wafted out over the waves, which they mistake for the fields of the chalky landscape, searching them for flowers. On a day such as this, the land, reflected in the sea, appears to enter into the sea, as though it lies under it, like Atlantis. The wires of the harp are like a seen music fusing seascape and landscape.

Looking at this vision in another way, it obviously has symbolic value. The sea represents death and eternity, the land represents the brief life of the summer and of one human generation which passes into the sea of eternity. But let me here say at once that although the poet may be conscious of this aspect of his vision, it is exactly what he wants to avoid stating, or even being too concerned with. His job is to recreate his vision, and let it speak its moral for itself. The poet must distinguish clearly in his own mind between that which most definitely must be said and that which must not be said. The unsaid inner meaning is revealed in the music and the tonality of the poem, and the poet is conscious of it in his knowledge that a certain tone of voice, a certain rhythm, are necessary.

In the next twenty versions of the poem I felt my way towards the clarification of the seen picture, the music and the inner feeling. In the first version quoted above, there is the phrase in the second and third lines

The waves
Like wires burn with the sun's copper glow.

This phrase fuses the image of the sea with the idea of music, and it is therefore a key-phrase, because the theme of the poem is the fusion of the land with the sea. Here, then are several versions of these one and a quarter lines, in the order in which they were written:

b)   The waves are wires
  Burning as with the secret song of fires

c) The day burns in the trembling wires
  With a vast music golden in the eyes

d) The day glows on its trembling wires
  Singing a golden music in the eyes

e) The day glows on its burning wires
  Like waves of music golden to the eyes.

f)   Afternoon burns upon its wires
     Lines of music dazzling the eyes

g)   Afternoon gilds its tingling wires
     To a visual silent music of the eyes

In the final version, these two lines appear as in the following stanza:

h)   There are some days the happy ocean lies
     Like an unfingered harp, below the land.

     Afternoon gilds all the silent wires
     Into a burning music of the eyes.

     On mirroring paths between those fine-strung fires
     The shore, laden with roses, horses, spires,
     Wanders in water, imaged above ribbed sand.

INSPIRATION

The hard work evinced in these examples, which are only a fraction of the work put into the whole poem, may cause the reader to wonder whether there is no such thing as inspiration, or whether it is merely Stephen Spender who is uninspired. The answer is that everything in poetry is work except inspiration, whether this work is achieved at one swift stroke, as Mozart wrote his music, or whether it is a slow process of evolution from stage to stage. Here again, I have to qualify the word "work," as I qualified the word "concentration": the work on a line of poetry may take the form of putting a version aside for a few days, weeks or years, and then taking it up again, when it may be found that the line has, in the interval of time, almost rewritten itself.

Inspiration is the beginning of a poem and it is also its final goal. It is the first idea which drops into the poet's mind and it is the final idea which he at last achieves in words. In between this start and this winning post there is the hard race, the sweat and toil.

Paul Valéry speaks of the *"une ligne donnée"* of a poem. One line is given to the poet by God or by nature, the rest he has to discover for himself.

My own experience of inspiration is certainly that of a line or a phrase or a word or sometimes something still vague, a dim cloud of an idea which I feel must be condensed into a shower of words. The peculiarity of the key word or line is that it does not merely attract, as, say, the word "braggadocio" attracts. It occurs in what seems to be an active, male, germinal form as though it were the center of a statement requiring a beginning and an end, and as though it had an impulse in a certain direction. Here are examples:

A language of flesh and roses

This phrase (not very satisfactory in itself) brings to my mind a whole series of experiences and the idea of a poem which I shall perhaps write some years hence. I was standing in the corridor of a train passing through the Black Country. I saw a landscape of pits and pitheads, artificial mountains, jagged yellow wounds in the earth, everything transformed as though by the toil of an enormous animal or giant tearing up the earth in search of prey or treasure. Oddly enough, a stranger next to me in the corridor echoed my inmost thought. He said: "Everything there is man-made." At this moment the line flashed into my head

A language of flesh and roses

The sequence of my thought was as follows: the industrial landscape, which seems by now a routine and act of God which enslaves both employers and workers who serve and profit by it, is actually the expression of man's will. Men willed it to be so, and the pitheads, slag-heaps, and the ghastly disregard of anything but the pursuit of wealth are a symbol of modern man's mind. In other words, the world which we create —the world of slums and telegrams and newspapers—is a kind of language of our inner wishes and thoughts. Although this is so, it is obviously a language which has got outside our control. It is a confused language, an irresponsible senile gibberish. This thought greatly distressed me, and I started thinking that if the phenomena created by humanity are really like words in a language, what kind of language do we really aspire to? All this sequence of thought flashed into my mind with the answer which came before the question: *A language of flesh and roses.*

I hope this example will give the reader some idea of what I mean by inspiration. Now the line, which I shall not repeat again, is a way of thinking imaginatively. If the line embodies some of the ideas which I have related above, these ideas must be further made clear in other lines. That is the terrifying challenge of poetry. Can I think out the logic of images? How easy it is to explain here the poem that I would have liked to write! How difficult it would be to write it. For writing it would imply living my way through the imaged experience of all these ideas, which here are mere abstractions, and such an effort of imaginative experience requires a lifetime of patience and watching.

Here is an example of a cloudy form of thought germinated by the word *cross,* which is the key word of the poem which exists formlessly in my mind. Recently my wife had a son. On the first day that I visited her after the boy's birth, I went by bus to the hospital. Passing through the streets on the top of the bus, they all seemed very clean, and the thought occurred to me that everything was prepared for our child. Past generations have toiled so that any child born today inherits, with his generation, cities, streets, organization, the most elaborate machinery for living. Everything has been provided for him by people dead long before he was born. Then, naturally enough, sadder thoughts colored this picture for me, and I reflected how he also inherited vast maladjustments, vast human wrongs. Then I thought of the child as like a pinpoint of present existence, the moment incarnate, in whom the whole of the past, and all possible futures *cross.* This word *cross* somehow suggested the whole situation to me of a child born into the world and also of the form of a poem about his situation. When the word *cross* appeared in the poem, the idea of the past should give place to the idea of the future and it should be apparent that the *cross* in which present and future meet is the secret of an individual human existence. And here again, the unspoken secret which lies beyond the poem, the moral significance of other meanings of the word "cross" begins to glow with its virtue that should never be said and yet should shine through every image in the poem.

This account of inspiration is probably weak beside the accounts that other poets might give. I am writing of my own experience, and my own inspiration seems to me like the faintest flash of insight into the nature of reality beside that of other poets whom I can think of. However, it is possible that I describe here a kind of experience which, however slight it may be, is far truer to the real poetic experience than Aldous Huxley's account of how a young poet writes poetry in his novel *Time Must Have a Stop.* It is hard to imagine anything more self-conscious and unpoetic than Mr. Huxley's account.

MEMORY

If the art of concentrating in a particular way is the discipline necessary for poetry to reveal itself, memory exercised in a particular way is the natural gift of poetic genius. The poet, above all else, is a person who never forgets certain sense-impressions which he has experienced and which he can relive again and again as though with all their original freshness.

All poets have this highly developed sensitive apparatus of memory, and they are usually aware of experiences which happened to them at the earliest age and which retain their pristine significance throughout life. The meeting of Dante and Beatrice when the poet was only nine years of age is the experience which became a symbol in Dante's mind around which the *Divine Comedy* crystallized. The experience of nature which forms the subject of Wordsworth's poetry was an extension of a childhood vision of "natural presences" which surrounded the boy Wordsworth. And his decision in later life to live in the Lake District was a decision to return to the scene of these childhood memories which were the most important experiences in his poetry. There is evidence for the importance of this kind of memory in all the creative arts, and the argument certainly applies to prose which is creative. Sir Osbert Sitwell has told me that his book *Before the Bombardment,* which contains an extremely civilized and satiric account of the social life of Scarborough before and during the last war, was based on his observations of life in that resort before he had reached the age of twelve.

It therefore is not surprising that although I have no memory for telephone numbers, addresses, faces and where I have put this morning's correspondence, I have a perfect memory for the sensation of certain experiences which are crystallized for me around certain associations. I could demonstrate this from my own life by the overwhelming nature of associations which, suddenly aroused, have carried me back so completely into the past, particularly into my childhood, that I have lost all sense of the present time and place. But the best proofs of this power of memory are found in the odd lines of poems written in notebooks fifteen years ago. A few fragments of unfinished poems enable me to enter immediately into the experiences from which they were derived, the circumstances in which they were written, and the unwritten feelings in the poem that were projected but never put into words.

> . . . Knowledge of a full sun
> That runs up his big sky, above
> The hill, then in those trees and throws
> His smiling on the turf.

That is an incomplete idea of fifteen years ago, and I remember exactly a balcony of a house facing a road, and, on the other side of the road, pine trees, beyond which lay the sea. Every morning the sun sprang

up, first of all above the horizon of the sea, then it climbed to the tops
of the trees and shone on my window. And this memory connects with
the sun that shines through my window in London now in spring and
early summer. So that the memory is not exactly a memory. It is more
like one prong upon which a whole calendar of similar experiences
happening throughout years collect. A memory once clearly stated ceases
to be a memory, it becomes perpetually present, because every time we
experience something which recalls it, the clear and lucid original experience imposes its formal beauty on the new experiences. It is thus
no longer a memory but an experience lived through again and again.

Turning over these old notebooks, my eye catches some lines, in a
projected long poem, which immediately reshape themselves into the
following short portrait of a woman's face:

> Her eyes are gleaming fish
> Caught in her nervous face, as if in a net.
> Her hair is wild and fair, haloing her cheeks
> Like a fantastic flare of Southern sun.
> There is madness in her cherishing her children.
> Sometimes, perhaps a single time in years,
> Her wandering fingers stoop to arrange some flowers—
> Then in her hands her whole life stops and weeps.

It is perhaps true to say that memory is the faculty of poetry, because
the imagination itself is an exercise of memory. There is nothing we
imagine which we do not already know. And our ability to imagine
is our ability to remember what we have already once experienced and
to apply it to some different situation. Thus the greatest poets are those
with memories so great that they extend beyond their strongest experiences to their minutest observations of people and things far outside
their own self-centeredness (the weakness of memory is its self-centeredness: hence the narcissistic nature of most poetry).

Here I can detect my own greatest weakness. My memory is defective
and self-centered. I lack the confidence in using it to create situations
outside myself, although I believe that, in theory, there are very few
situations in life which a poet should not be able to imagine, because it
is a fact that most poets have experienced almost every situation in life.
I do not mean by this that a poet who writes about a polar expedition
has actually been to the North Pole. I mean, though, that he has been
cold, hungry, etc., so that it is possible for him by remembering imaginatively his own felt experiences to know what it is like to explore the

North Pole. That is where I fail. I cannot write about going to the North Pole.

FAITH

It is evident that a faith in their vocation, mystical in intensity, sustains poets. There are many illustrations from the lives of poets to show this, and Shakespeare's sonnets are full of expressions of his faith in the immortality of his lines.

From my experience I can clarify the nature of this faith. When I was nine, we went to the Lake District, and there my parents read me some of the poems of Wordsworth. My sense of the sacredness of the task of poetry began then, and I have always felt that a poet's was a sacred vocation, like a saint's. Since I was nine, I have wanted to be various things, for example, Prime Minister (when I was twelve). Like some other poets I am attracted by the life of power and the life of action, but I am still more repelled by them. Power involves forcing oneself upon the attention of historians by doing things and occupying offices which are, in themselves, important, so that what is truly powerful is not the soul of a so-called powerful and prominent man but the position which he fills and the things which he does. Similarly, the life of "action" which seems so very positive is, in fact, a selective, even a negative kind of life. A man of action does one thing or several things because he does not do something else. Usually men who do very spectacular things fail completely to do the ordinary things which fill the lives of most normal people, and which would be far more heroic and spectacular perhaps, if they did not happen to be done by many people. Thus in practice the life of action has always seemed to me an act of cutting oneself off from life.

Although it is true that poets are vain and ambitious, their vanity and ambition is of the purest kind attainable in this world, for the saint renounces ambition. They are ambitious to be accepted for what they ultimately are as revealed by their inmost experiences, their finest perceptions, their deepest feelings, their uttermost sense of truth, in their poetry. They cannot cheat about these things, because the quality of their own being is revealed not in the noble sentiments which their poetry expresses, but in sensibility, control of language, rhythm and music, things which cannot be attained by a vote of confidence from an electorate, or by the office of Poet Laureate. Of course, work is tremendously important, but, in poetry, even the greatest labor can only serve to reveal the intrinsic qualities of soul of the poet as he really is.

Since there can be no cheating, the poet, like the saint, stands in all his works before the bar of a perpetual day of judgment. His vanity of course is pleased by success, though even success may contribute to his understanding that popularity does not confer on him the favorable judgment of all the ages which he seeks. For what does it mean to be praised by one's own age, which is soaked in crimes and stupidity, except perhaps that future ages, wise where we are foolish, will see him as a typical expression of this age's crimes and stupidity? Nor is lack of success a guarantee of great poetry, though there are some who pretend that it is. Nor can the critics, at any rate beyond a certain limited point of technical judgment, be trusted.

The poet's faith is therefore, firstly, a mystique of vocation, secondly, a faith in his own truth, combined with his own devotion to a task. There can really be no greater faith than the confidence that one is doing one's utmost to fulfill one's high vocation, and it is this that has inspired all the greatest poets. At the same time this faith is coupled with a deep humility because one knows that, ultimately, judgment does not rest with oneself. All one can do is to achieve nakedness, to be what one is with all one's faculties and perceptions, strengthened by all the skill which one can acquire, and then to stand before the judgment of time.

In my notebooks, I find the following Prose Poem, which expresses these thoughts:

> Bring me peace bring me power bring me assurance. Let me reach the bright day, the high chair, the plain desk, where my hand at last controls the words, where anxiety no longer undermines me. If I don't reach these I'm thrown to the wolves, I'm a restless animal wandering from place to place, from experience to experience.
>
> Give me the humility and the judgment to live alone with the deep and rich satisfaction of my own creating: not to be thrown into doubt by a word of spite or disapproval.
>
> In the last analysis don't mind whether your work is good or bad so long as it has the completeness, the enormity of the whole world which you love.

SONG

Inspiration and song are the irreducible final qualities of a poet which make his vocation different from all others. Inspiration is an experience in which a line or an idea is given to one, and perhaps also a state of

mind in which one writes one's best poetry. Song is far more difficult to
define. It is the music which a poem as yet unthought of will assume,
the empty womb of poetry forever in the poet's consciousness, waiting
for the fertilizing seed.

Sometimes, when I lie in a state of half-waking half-sleeping, I am
conscious of a stream of words which seem to pass through my mind,
without their having a meaning, but they have a sound, a sound of
passion, or a sound recalling poetry that I know. Again sometimes when
I am writing, the music of the words I am trying to shape takes me far
beyond the words, I am aware of a rhythm, a dance, a fury, which is
as yet empty of words.

In these observations, I have said little about headaches, midnight oil,
pints of beer or of claret, love affairs, and so on, which are supposed to
be stations on the journeys of poets through life. There is no doubt that
writing poetry, when a poem appears to succeed, results in an intense
physical excitement, a sense of release and ecstasy. On the other hand,
I dread writing poetry, for, I suppose, the following reasons: a poem
is a terrible journey, a painful effort of concentrating the imagination;
words are an extremely difficult medium to use, and sometimes when
one has spent days trying to say a thing clearly one finds that one has
only said it dully; above all, the writing of a poem brings one face to
face with one's own personality with all its familiar and clumsy limitations. In every other phase of existence, one can exercise the orthodoxy
of a conventional routine: one can be polite to one's friends, one can
get through the day at the office, one can pose, one can draw attention
to one's position in society, one is—in a word—dealing with men. In
poetry, one is wrestling with a god.

Usually, when I have completed a poem, I think "this is my best
poem," and I wish to publish it at once. This is partly because I only
write when I have something new to say, which seems more worth while
than what I have said before, partly because optimism about my present
and future makes me despise my past. A few days after I have finished
a poem, I relegate it to the past of all my other wasted efforts, all the
books I do not wish to open.

Perhaps the greatest pleasure I have gotten from poems that I have
written is when I have heard some lines quoted which I have not at
once recognized. And I have thought "how good and how interesting,"
before I have realized that they are my own.

In common with other creative writers I pretend that I am not, and

I am, exceedingly affected by unsympathetic criticism, whilst praise usually makes me suspect that the reviewer does not know what he is talking about. Why are writers so sensitive to criticism? Partly, because it is their business to be sensitive, and they are sensitive about this as about other things. Partly, because every serious creative writer is really in his heart concerned with reputation and not with success (the most successful writer I have known, Sir Hugh Walpole, was far and away the most unhappy about his reputation, because the "highbrows" did not like him). Again, I suspect that every writer is secretly writing for *someone,* probably for a parent or teacher who did not believe in him in childhood. The critic who refuses to "understand" immediately becomes identified with this person, and the understanding of many admirers only adds to the writer's secret bitterness if this one refusal persists.

Gradually one realizes that there is always this someone who will not like one's work. Then, perhaps, literature becomes a humble exercise of faith in being all that one can be in one's art, of being more than oneself, expecting little, but with a faith in the mystery of poetry which gradually expands into a faith in the mysterious service of truth.

Yet what failures there are! And how much mud sticks to one; mud not thrown by other people but acquired in the course of earning one's living, answering or not answering the letters which one receives, supporting or not supporting public causes. All one can hope is that this mud is composed of little grains of sand which will produce pearls.

THE DOCTRINE

OF INTERNAL

NECESSITY

WASSILY KANDINSKY

The effects we receive, which often appear chaotic, consist of three elements: the action of the color of the object, of its form, and of the object per se, independent of either color or form.

At this point the individuality of the artist asserts itself and makes use of these three elements. Here too the purposive prevails. *It is clear, therefore, that the choice of an object (i.e., one of the elements of form) must be decided by a purposive vibration in the human soul; therefore, the choice of the object also originates from the principle of internal necessity.*

The freer the abstract form, the purer and more primitive the vibration. Therefore, in any composition where corporeal form seems superfluous it may be replaced by abstract or semi-abstract form. In each case this translation should be guided by our feeling. The more an

---

From Concerning the Spiritual in Art, *Documents of Modern Art, Vol. V* (*New York: George Wittenborn, Inc., 1955*). *Reprinted by permission of George Wittenborn, Inc.*

artist uses these semi-abstract or abstract forms, the deeper and more confidently will he advance into the sphere of the abstract. And after him will follow those who look at his pictures, who will in turn gradually acquire familiarity with the language of abstract art.

Must we then altogether abandon representation and work solely in abstraction? The problem of harmonizing the appeal of the concrete and the abstract answers this question. Just as each spoken word rouses an internal vibration, so does every object represented. To deprive oneself of this possibility of causing a vibration would be reducing one's arsenal of means of expression: anyhow, that is the case today. But besides this, there is another one which art can always offer to any question beginning with "must": There is no "must" in art, because art is always free.

With regard to the second problem of composition, the creation of the forms which are to compose the whole, it must be remembered that the same form with the same relations will always have the same internal appeal. Only the relations constantly vary. The result is that: (1) Ideal harmony alters according to its relation with other forms; (2) Even in similar relations, a slight approach to or withdrawal from other forms may affect the structure.[1] Nothing is absolute. Form composition is relative, depending on (1) alterations in the relations of one form to another, and (2) alterations in each individual form, down to the very smallest. Every form is as sensitive as smoke, the slightest wind will fundamentally alter it. This extreme mobility makes it perhaps easier to obtain similar harmonies from the use of different forms than from a repetition of the same one: apart from the fact that, of course, an exact repetition can never be produced. So long as we are susceptible mainly to the appeal of a whole composition, this fact is of theoretical importance. But when we become more sensitive, by a constant use of abstract forms (which have no material interpretation), it will become of great practical significance. On the one hand, the difficulties of art will increase, but at the same time the wealth of forms of expression will also increase in quality and quantity. Simultaneously the problem of distortion in drawing disappears and is replaced by the problem of how far the internal structure of a particular form is veiled or bared. This changed point of view will lead further and to greater enrichment of the media of expression because veiling is of enormous power in art.

---

[1] This is what we mean when we speak of "movement." For example, an upright triangle is more steadfast and quiet than one set obliquely on the surface.

The combining of the veiled and bared will form a new possibility of *leitmotivs* in form composition.

Without such development as this, form composition is impossible. To anyone who cannot experience the internal structure of form (whether natural or abstract), composition must be meaningless and arbitrary. Apparently aimless alterations in arrangement make art seem a senseless game of forms. Here we find the same criterion and principle which thus far we have encountered everywhere as the only purely artistic one free from the unessential, *the principle of inner necessity*.

If, for example, features of the face or parts of the body are changed or distorted for artistic reasons, one encounters not only the purely pictorial question but also that of anatomy, which hampers the pictorial intention and imposes upon it the consideration of unimportant details. In our case, however, the unessential disappears automatically and only the essential remains, the artistic aim. These seemingly arbitrary but, in reality, well-reasoned alterations in form are one of the sources of an infinite number of artistic creations.

The flexibility of each form, its internal, organic variation, its direction (motion) in the picture, the relative weight of concrete or of abstract forms and their combination; further, the concord or discord of the various elements of a pictorial structure, the handling of groups, the combination of the hidden and the stripped bare, the use of rhythmical or unrhythmical, or geometrical or nongeometrical forms, their contiguity or separation—all these things are the elements of structure in drawing.

But as long as color is excluded, such structure is confined to black and white. Color itself offers contrapuntal possibilities and, when combined with design, may lead to the great pictorial counterpoint, where also painting achieves composition, and where pure art is in the service of the divine. The same infallible guide will carry it to the great heights, *the principle of internal necessity*.

Inner necessity originates from three elements: (1) Every artist, as a creator, has something in him which demands expression (this is the element of personality). (2) Every artist, as the child of his time, is impelled to express the spirit of his age (this is the element of style)— dictated by the period and particular country to which the artist belongs (it is doubtful how long the latter distinction will continue). (3) Every artist, as a servant of art, has to help the cause of art (this is the

quintessence of art, which is constant in all ages and among all nation-
alities).

A full understanding of the first two elements is necessary for a realization of the third. But he who realizes this will recognize that a rudely
carved Indian column is an expression of the spirit that actuates any
advance-guard work.

There has been in the past, and there is now, much talk of "personality" in art. Talk of the coming "style" is more frequent each day.
But in spite of their importance now, these questions will lose their
edge under the perspective of time.

Only the third element—that of quintessential art—will remain forever. Time, far from diminishing its importance, increases it. An Egyp-
tian carving moves us more deeply today than it did its contemporaries;
for they judged it with the restrictive knowledge of period and personality. But we can judge it as an expression of an eternal art.

Similarly, the greater the part played in a modern work of art by the
elements of style and personality, the better will it be appreciated by
people today; but a modern work of art which is full of the third element will fail to reach the contemporary soul. Sometimes centuries
have to pass before the third element is understood. But the artist in
whose work this third element predominates is the great artist.

These three mystical necessities are the constituent elements of a work
of art, which interpenetrate and constitute unity of the work. Nevertheless, the first two elements include what belongs to time and space,
while in the pure and eternal artistry, which is beyond time and space,
this forms a relatively nontransparent shell. The process in the development in art consists of the separation of its quintessence from the style
of the time and the element of personality. Thus, these two elements are
not only a cooperative but also a hindering force. The personality and
the style of the time create in every epoch many precise forms, which in
spite of apparent major differences are so organically related that they
can be designated as one single form: their inner sound is finally but one
major chord. These two elements are of a subjective nature. The entire
epoch desires to reflect itself, to express artistically its life. Likewise, the
artist wishes to express himself and chooses only forms which are sympathetic to his inner self. Thus, gradually is formed the style of an
epoch, i.e., a certain external and subjective form. The pure and eternal
art is, however, the objective element which becomes comprehensible
with the help of the subjective.

The inevitable desire for expression of the *objective* is the impulse here defined as "internal necessity." This impulse is the lever or spring driving the artist forward. Because the spirit progresses, today's internal laws of harmony are tomorrow's external laws, which in their further application live only through this necessity which has become external. It is clear, therefore, that the inner spirit of art uses the external form of any particular period as a stepping-stone to further development.

In short, the effect of internal necessity and the development of art is an ever advancing expression of the eternal and objective in terms of the historical and subjective.

Because the objective is forever exchanging the subjective expression of today for that of the morrow, each new extension of liberty in the use of external form is hailed as final and supreme. At present we say that an artist may use any form, so long as he draws on forms that exist in nature. But this limitation, like all its predecessors, is temporary. From the point of view of inner need, no limitation can be made. The artist may use any form which his expression demands; his inner impulse must find suitable external form.

Thus one sees finally (and this is of utmost importance for today or any time) that to seek for personality and "style," for nationality, to achieve this deliberately, is not only impossible but comparatively unimportant. The general relationship of those works of art, which through the centuries are not weakened but always more and more strengthened, does not lie in the "external" but in the deep roots of mystical inner content. Therefore, the following of schools, the searching for the "mode," the desire for principles in a work and the insistence upon certain media of expression of a period can only be misleading and must bring misunderstanding, obscurity and silence.

The artist must ignore distinctions between "recognized" or "unrecognized" conventions of form, the transitory knowledge and demands of his particular age. He must watch his own inner life and hearken to the demands of internal necessity. Then he may safely employ means sanctioned or forbidden by his contemporaries. This is the only way to express the mystical necessity. All means are sacred which are called for by internal necessity. All means are sinful which are not drawn from inner necessity.

It is impossible to theorize about this ideal. In real art, theory does not precede practice but follows it. Everything is at first a matter of feeling. Even though the general structure may be formulated theoretically, there is still an additional something which constitutes the soul of creation. Any theoretical scheme will be lacking in the essential of creation—the internal desire for expression—which cannot be formulated. Despite the most accurate weights and balances to be had, a purely deductive weighing can never suffice. True proportions cannot be calculated, nor true scales be found ready-made.[2] Proportions and scales are not outside the artist but within him; they are what we may call a feeling for boundaries, artistic tact—qualities which are innate and which may be raised by enthusiasm to genius. In this sense we may understand the possibility of a general base to painting, as envisaged by Goethe. Such a grammar of painting is at present a matter of conjecture, and, should it ever be achieved, it will be not so much according to physical laws (which have often been tried and which the cubists try today), as according to the laws of internal necessity, which is of the soul.

---

[2] The many-sided genius of Leonardo devised a system of little spoons with which different colors were to be used, thus creating a kind of mechanical harmony. One of his pupils, after trying in vain to use this system, in despair asked one of his colleagues how the master himself used the invention. The colleague replied: "The master never uses it at all" [Dmitri Merejkowski, *The Romance of Leonardo da Vinci,* B. G. Guerney, trans. (New York: Heritage Press, 1954)].

CREATION—

ARTISTIC, NATURAL,

AND DIVINE

ETIENNE GILSON

In speaking of creation, no artist normally imagines himself a rival of the supreme being Paul Cézanne used to call *Deus Pater Omnipotens*. Some artists may have been tempted by pride, but few succumbed to the temptation. Yet the sole fact that such an illusion was at least possible proves that the making of works of art implies a feeling of power and of domination over matter analogous to those which religion attributed to God. We have noted several expressions of this creative exaltation written by various painters, but some of them have carried their observation deeper and attempted to say in what sense, although the formula could not be taken as literally true, they felt justified in describing their work as creation.

Seen from without, works of art are characterized by their amazing diversity. Civilizations, countries, schools, individual artists, all leave

From Painting and Reality, *Bollingen Series XXXV* (*New York: Pantheon Books, Inc., 1957*). *Reprinted by permission of the Bollingen Foundation.*

behind paintings recognizable by their styles and bearing the marks of
their various origins. Seen from within—that is, from the point of view
of their authors—these paintings are characterized by their imprevisibility. Naturally, history does not hesitate to explain how, and for what
reasons, the art of painting has followed the evolution that it has taken.
What has not yet been seen is a painter able to foretell the future evolution of his art or the probable development of his own career, or even,
when he begins a new painting, what this particular work will look like
after being completed. Unless we are mistaken, what the term "creation"
expresses in the writings of artists is precisely that character of "novelty" which is so typical of artistic production. Far from proceeding
with the mechanical previsibility of natural operations, whose effects are
always more or less previsible and, as they say, determined, art is full
of ignorances, uncertainties, and surprises for the artist himself, who
sometimes sees his work docilely following his decisions, sometimes
entering ways he had not foreseen.

These two characteristics of imprevisibility and liberty are the more
remarkable in that, according to the unanimous consent of painters,
nothing is more dangerous for them than to trust to luck. The kind of
imprevisibility that characterizes the work of art is very different from
that which attends chance. No true artist will leave anything to chance;
only, when everything has been foreseen, prepared, and calculated, the
creative painter still does not know what his work is going to be. What
he has calculated is less his work than the way he is going to do it. An
artist somewhat resembles a man who, before making a decision of vital
importance, collects all the facts relevant to the case, weighs the various
decisions that are possible, calculates their probable consequences, and
still does not know how his will ultimately will decide. These are the
classical moments of the philosophical description of a free act. Just as
previsibility attends determination, imprevisibility attends liberty. The
true meaning of the word "creation" in the writings of painters is prac-
tically the same as that of the word "liberty" when it is understood in
this sense. As Eric Gill once said, the artist does not create *de nihilo*,
but he does create *de novo*. This is so true that when we want to say
of an artist that he has had his day, we simply say that he is unable
to renew himself. A self-repeating artist has reached the end of his
creative activity.[1]

Remarkably enough, the questions we ask about the probable future

---

[1] "Plato's theory is right enough but does not go *all* the way. The word 'type'
suggests one thing which is typical of many things. No doubt this is an important
department of 'art'—the discovery of the *type*, the weeding out of the accidental

of a painter's career, or, for that matter, about the probable future of the art of painting in general, are similar to the questions an observer could have asked, many millenniums ago, concerning the probable development of life on the surface of the earth. Even now, confronted with the results of these millenniums of change, modern science does not find it too easy to explain how this change took place. The word "evolution" remains a symbol for a demonstrated explanation still to come. We simply do not know.[2] But if it is true that man is part and parcel of nature, and that artists are men, then their personal experience of artistic creativity should be able to unveil to us some of the secrets of the inventiveness of nature. Unless we decide that man is unrelated to the cosmos in which he lives, what happens in him must bear some relationship to what is happening to the whole of which he is a part. What happens in painters suggests the presence, at the origin of universal becoming, of an inner force of invention and creativity that, everywhere at work in the world of matter, achieves self-awareness in the minds of artists.

This approach to the cosmic problems discussed by scientists and philosophers is neglected by almost all philosophers. The reason for this is that philosophy itself is knowledge, and since knowledge must be true to exist, philosophical problems are usually related to the truth of certain propositions. Now, truth is the conformity of intellection with its object. Consequently, where there is no object, there is no truth. This

---

& extraneous so that, as in a Hindu sculpture of a tree, all trees are resumed. But this job is only one department & not I think the *most* important—it is one of the arts but not the highest or most specifically artistic art so to say. The art which is art specifically & at its highest is that of pure creation—*de novo, ad hoc & ex nihilo.* This is God's art & not man's. But man, in the second degree, by virtue of 'free will' can create (not out of nothing, but, *de novo & ad hoc,* out of what God has made). Thus he makes not types but *uniques*— things that represent nothing but themselves & of which there is & cannot be another example in the whole Universe of created beings." *Letters of Eric Gill,* Walter Shewring, ed. (New York: The Devin-Adair Company, 1948), p. 235; cf., pp. 275f.

[2] Biological evolution is a fact; what still remains obscure are the limits of this fact as well as the reasons that make it different from mere change. There is, as biologists say, "orthogenesis"—that is, "the process by which a certain number of characteristics are modified in evolution in the same direction and according to a principle of increasing unity" [Jean-Paul Aron, "The Problem of Evolution," *Diogenes,* Vol. VII (1954), 94, n. 5]. This is what remains to be accounted for—namely, the very fact, known to all those who ever considered the most elementary facts in embryogency, and which Aristotle explained by the notion of final cause.—On the present scientific formulation of these problems, see L. Cuenot, *L'Evolution biologique* (Paris: Masson, 1951). His conclusions are summed up in Jean-Paul Aron, *op. cit.* 96.

consequence entails another one. If there are forces or energies in the world whose operations cause effects that are new in both existence and nature, philosophers feel naturally inclined to disregard them as irrelevant to their own discipline. In this, science in no way differs from philosophy. Always ready to account for works of art, and even for artists, once artists have already produced their works, science is unable to say anything sensible about the very act by which works of art are being produced by artists. Some painters have been so acutely aware of the opposition between the respective attitudes of artists and scientists toward reality that they expressed their dislike of scientists in somewhat crude terms.[3] But there is no opposition between art and science; there simply is a real distinction between their functions. The very possibility of science presupposes the existence of realities produced by art, or by a still higher power than that of artists and of art. By definition, science is not qualified to deal with what it presupposes. When science attempts to deal with what it itself naturally presupposes, it simply denies the existence of such problems or of such realities. The natural tendency of science and speculative philosophy is to consider their intellectual formulations of reality equivalent to reality itself. True enough, philosophers and scientists are well aware of the fact that they do not know everything; on the contrary, they often declare that what they know is little in comparison with what still remains to be known; but they also believe that what remains to be known will be found to be homogeneous in nature with what they already know.

If there are forces or energies in the world productive of novelty, the only discipline that can directly communicate with them is art, any art, provided only it keeps faith with its own essence, which is that of a creative activity in the order of formal being. When approached from the point of view of art, reality becomes very different from what it seems to be when seen from the point of view of speculation. It is being only to the extent that becoming is being. Art introduces us to a world of forms whose final completion is the outcome of a sort of biological growth.[4] But even this is not quite true, for biological growth does not

---

[3] See the comic hostility of Delacroix toward scientists in general, *The Journal of Eugene Delacroix*, Walter Pach, trans. (New York: Covici, Friede, Inc., 1937), pp. 155f.

[4] Art imitates nature (Aristotle, *Physics*, II, 2, 194a, 21). This saying is usually understood in the sense that the works of art strive to imitate the visual appearance of the works of nature. This is not what it means in Aristotle; the art he has in mind is medicine, which works as nature does. As Thomas Aquinas understands it, this famous saying means that art is to its operations and its works in the same relationship as nature is to its own operations and its own

seem to have any choice, whereas artists are in quest of forms that only their own free choice is able to determine. Nor should we feel surprised to hear some of them describe their attitude as one of obedience to an "internal necessity," for, indeed, the long and ascetic preparation that precedes artistic creation has precisely for its object to eliminate the obstacles—perceptions, images, imitational urges, acquired habits, and even skill—that stand in the way of the new germinal form and impede its materialization. The internal necessity to which an artist must submit is not a necessity for his will. The internal necessity by which creative artists often feel bound is that of the very form to which their own free will chooses to give actual existence in a matter fittingly disposed to receive it. Other disciplines, such as, for instance, ethics, can introduce philosophers to the problems related to the freedom of doing; art is the only approach we have to the freedom of making.

This is to say that art invites philosophy to take into serious consideration problems for which philosophers exhibit little interest.[5] In Plato's doctrine, all questions related to existence as well as to the causes and origins of things are kept out of the domain of science properly so called and reserved for probable opinion, which expresses itself under the form of narratives, or myths. Plato's *Timaeus* is the

---

works. The whole doctrine has been summarized as follows: "The origin of what is made by art is the human intellect, itself derived, as some sort of resemblance, from the divine intellect, which is the origin of natural things. Whence it necessarily follows that the operations of art imitate the operations of nature, and also that the products of art imitate the products of nature." Man looks at the way God does things in nature in order to learn, as a good pupil, how to do his own works; but the two domains remain distinct because the works of nature are no works of art. "If art had to make things of nature, it would operate as nature does. But, on the one hand, nature does not bring any work of art to completion; it simply prepares certain of their elements and places under the eyes of artists, so to speak, a model of the way to operate. On the other hand, art may well examine the products of nature; it even can make use of them in order to perform its own works, but it cannot produce the works of nature. Whence it appears that with respect to the things of nature, human reason does nothing more than to *know;* but with respect to works of art, human reason both *knows* and *makes* ["est et cognoscitiva et factiva"]. Thus, those among the human sciences which are about natural objects are speculative, whereas those which are about man-made things are practical, and about operations carried in imitation of nature." [Thomas Aquinas, *In libros politicorum Aristotelis expositio,* Prooemium, 1-2 (ed. Spiazzi, p. 1).]—The doctrine is sometimes expressed in saying that art imitates nature in operation rather than in representation: "ars imitatur naturam in operando, non in repraesentando."

[5] Our own views on this philosophical problem are to be found in *Being and Some Philosophers,* 2nd ed. (Toronto: Pontifical Institute of Mediaeval Studies, 1952).

best example of such an approach to these problems. In the philosophy of Aristotle, on the contrary, there are no such things as myths, so all problems related to origins disappear at once. The world of Aristotle is eternal, indestructible, as well as uncreated, and all the fleeting beings that ceaselessly come to be and pass away are nothing more than temporary embodiments of their eternal and immutable species. Only the accidental is new in the world of Aristotle; it is no wonder, then, that when the time came for him to define art, he found nothing better to say about it than to reduce it to imitation. What else could he have done? Both philosophy and science are hostile to becoming, except, of course, to the becoming that brings nothing really new into the world and does not endanger previsibility.

Theology has often favored similar views, for the simple reason that, since they had to credit God with science, many theologians naturally conceived him by analogy with a perfect human scientist. But there were difficulties. The first one was that, since Aristotle had not had to solve any problem of origins, he had had no use for the notion of Ideas. It thus became imperative for theologians to supplement Aristotle with Plato. Now, this simply cannot be done. Philosophies just are not that way. One cannot possibly retain ninety-five per cent of Aristotle and add five per cent of Plato to it. If one does, the resulting mixture is plain incoherence. So theologians have had no other choice than to evolve their own notion of the creative power of God and of the way in which this power has been exercised. This has led them to two conclusions that, rather hard to reconcile from the point of view of man, must needs be actually reconciled, in fact, if there is a God. One of these conclusions is that, since the divine science must needs be perfect, the future of the universe must eternally remain an open book before the sight of God. The second one is that, since there are freedom and contingency in the universe, the perfect knowledge that God has of the future does not prevent contingency and freedom from playing their parts in the general history of the world. Various theological answers have been given to this essentially theological problem; the only point we are concerned with, as philosophers, is the fact that an exclusively speculative approach to the problem is bound to minimize the elements of novelty and natural imprevisibility which must be present in a world created by the free will of an all-powerful God. The reason for this assertion can be stated in a few words: if all effects resemble their causes, a freely created world must exhibit at least some traces of the free creative power of its Author.

This is the reason why, despite resemblances in terminologies, the created universe of Christian theologians has never been identical with the uncreated universe of Aristotle; but the same reason probably accounts for this other fact, that when modern artists undertook to investigate the nature of their own activity, they spontaneously resorted to the creationist terminology of Christian theologians. As often happens, while speculating in the light of its own principles, theology is here acting as a guiding star for philosophers considering the nature of the world as well as for artists considering the nature of art.

If there is such a thing as a divine art, it must be very different from our own. First of all, our own art never creates in the proper sense of the word. It does not create its matter; it does not even properly create its forms. Human art simply assembles the elements of composites that, once made, are possessed of their own forms for the sole reason that they *are*.[6] Moreover, if one can speak of God as of the supreme Artist, his art is certainly innocent of any groping and of any becoming due to what would be for him the incomplete previsibility of his own works. Unlike the Ideas of Plato, those of Christian theology are one with the very being of the Creator; unlike the Prime Mover of Aristotle, the Christian Creator of the world has Ideas of all things known by him and creatable by his power. For this very reason, nothing that happens can possibly be new in the sight of God. Yet, when all is said and done, the God of the Jews and of the Christians did create the universe, and if this was nothing new in him, it certainly was the beginning of all newness in the created world itself. According to Christian theology, creative power belongs to God alone, and the world of creation owns no parcel of it. But it does not take a divine power to achieve novelty in the communication of existence and in the forming of man-made beings. This is what artists do. It is what modern painting has done in the highest degree, and, be it for this reason only, it deserves the careful consideration of philosophers, even perhaps of theologians.

Metaphysicians and theologians usually say that, since effects resemble their causes, created beings resemble their Creator. Because his very essence is to be the pure act of being, the world created by God is, or exists. Because this existence of the world is due to the efficacy of the divine power acting as a cause, we see all the beings included in God's creation causing, acting, and operating in their diverse ways and according to their different natures. Things, Thomas Aquinas liked to say, imitate God in that they are and in that they are causes. Such are the

---

[6] Thomas Aquinas, *Summa Theologiae,* I, 45, 5, 1st obj. and answer.

painters, whose works add to the beauty of the world. Painters are the makers of new visual forms whose proper function is to make intelligibility perceptible to human sight.

This is the most solid ground there is for speaking of a religious art. In a created universe whatever exists is religious because it imitates God in its operations as well as in its being. If what precedes is true, art, too, is religious in its very essence, because to be creative is to imitate, in a finite and analogical way, the divine prerogative, exclusively reserved for HE WHO IS, of making things to be. Now, as has already been seen, to make things be and to make them beautiful are one and the same thing.[7] Each artist, then, while exerting his often anguished effort to add new types of beings to those which make up the world of nature, should be conscious of the resemblance between his finite art and the infinitely perfect efficacy of the divine power. All truly creative art is religious in its own right.

By the same token, the meaning of the words "Christian art" becomes at once apparent. The problem does not arise in connection with picturing conceived as an art distinct from painting properly so called. Some religions exclude images; others do not hesitate to appeal to them as to visual aids in the teaching of religious truth. Christianity has always done so, the more willingly as, upholding the truth of the substantial unity of man, the Church has always associated, in both cult and prayer, the mind of man, his affectivity, and his activity. It seems therefore evident that picturing fulfills in Christian worship an important function, whose proper end is inscribed in its very nature and which cannot possibly reach this end without resorting to imitational art. The subject here is of primary importance, and nothing is more legitimate in it than to do what most creative artists would consider an abomination: to rely upon the subject more than upon the art as a source of emotion. In religious imagery, this is not only legitimate; it is necessarily required by its very end. He to whom a bare wooden cross does not suffice is perhaps not so wholly Christian as he should be; he who sees in a crucifix the thing of beauty it may well be, but nothing else, is not a Christian at all. The art of doing Christian pictures does not exclude the possibility of doing Christian paintings; by itself, however, it necessarily is representational art.[8]

---

[7] The perfect formula is given by Eric Gill, *Beauty Looks After Herself* (London: Sheed & Ward, Ltd., 1933), p. 66: "Beauty—the word is a stumbling block. Do not let us stumble over it. Beauty is *the Splendour of Being*. The primary constituent of visible Being is Order."

[8] In his *Théories, 1890-1910, du symbolisme et de Gauguin vers un nouvel*

This answer is but indirectly related to the problem of creative Christian art. On the contrary, the fact that all the main moments of human life have a religious significance lies at the very center of the question. Ever since the birth of Our Lord, the birth of every child is a nativity. There is, in a Christian universe made up of created beings, a direct invitation to artists to join in the praise of God by cooperating with his creative power and by increasing, to the extent that man can do so, the sum total of being and beauty in the world. This is the more instantly required when the works to be produced by human art are primarily destined to a specifically religious use. There then is an inner affinity between the intended end and the means to be employed to reach it. Religion can survive without art; it even survives in spite of the fact that its churches have largely become so many temples dedicated to the exhibition of industrialized ugliness and to the veneration of painted nonbeing. But when Christian artists are called upon to celebrate the glory of God by cooperating, in their modest human manner, with the work of creation, it becomes imperative that their own works be things of beauty. Otherwise, these works would not truly *be,* and the artists themselves would contribute nothing.

Philosophers, too, have something to learn from a careful examination of art under all its forms. In the case of painting, we find ourselves enriched with privileged information concerning the way physical beings come to be. It would be somewhat naïve to imagine nature acting as an artist—that is to say, as a man—but the fear of this kind of anthropomorphism should not make us fall into another error, which consists in believing that man is in himself a separate being, self-sufficient and wholly different from the universe that includes him. The physical energies that move the world of matter crop up, so to speak, in man's self-awareness of himself as well as of his operations.

It is difficult for us, who are not sharing in their creative power, to formulate inferences based upon what artists say. There would be no

---

ordre classique (Paris: Bibliothèque de l'Occident, 1913), Maurice Denis strongly protested against the excesses of the "expression by the subject" in religious art. In 1896, he did not hesitate to write that, although a masterpiece, it was with Vinci's *Last Supper* that religious painting "entered the way to perdition." If he represents a subject endowed with an emotional value of its own, as was here the case, the painter does not act upon our emotions through his work, but through his subject. The way was then open to Munkácsy, Tissot, "and all that is worse in religious art." From then on, it was going to be the subject alone that, in religious painting, would invite to worship (pp. 41f). This perhaps is the shortest definition of the art Philistine: "He does not look at the painting; he sees nothing but the subject."

excuse for taking such liberties if they themselves were not so often found struggling for words in an effort to go beyond the limits of their own personal experience and to reach conclusions valid for all men. They do not all use the same formulas, but the diversity of their language points out a common truth for which perhaps there are no adequate words. The world in which creative painters live appears to them, not at all as an obstacle, but as something that must be transcended. Assuredly, for them as men, the world of nature is the very same reality it is for us and that we share in common with them, but for them as painters, it is not in the world of nature that ultimate reality lies. They feel that there is still another reality hidden behind the appearances of nature and that it is their own function to discover it in order to express it, or, rather, to express it in order to discover it; for, indeed, this metareality has to be made to be before being made to be known. The constantly recurring opposition of painters of all schools to the literal limitation of nature finds its deepest justification in this feeling. Nor is this conviction peculiar to painters alone. The "poetic principle" invoked by Edgar Allan Poe, which he simply calls "a sense of the Beautiful," seems to obey only one law—namely, not to be a mere repetition of the forms, the sounds, the odors of nature as well as of the common feelings with which they inspire all men.[9] When Poe says that "mere repetition is not poetry," he wholly agrees with the conviction expressed by so many painters that to initiate new realities, not to repeat already existing ones, is the proper end of the art of painting.

The universe in which painters live is therefore a still incomplete one. With a heart full of misgivings, the artist sees himself as one of those whom destiny has elected to enrich the world with new beings. Others before him have been honored with the same mission, and their works are there to witness their success in fulfilling it. But this is no reason he himself should evade his duty, for just as he could not have done the works of his predecessors, nobody else could possibly do the works he seems to be called upon to produce.

The force that will cause their existence is, first of all, an irresistible urge to paint probably akin to the fundamental forces that have given rise to the impressive procession of the vegetal and animal species since the first appearance of life upon earth. Despite its intensity, this force is neither a blind impulse nor a lucid progression toward a clearly seen goal. It could be more justly compared to the groping of primitive

---

[9] *The Complete Tales and Poems of Edgar Allen Poe,* Hervey Allen, ed. (New York: Modern Library, Inc., 1938), p. 893.

forms, if the forms of nature possessed an awareness of their own be-coming. A sort of inner sense of direction, not always immune to error, seems to direct both nature and artists toward their respective goals, which are the perfecting of one more being of nature or one more work of art.[10]

The most remarkable feature about this universe of creative artists is the particular relationship it reveals between being and intelligibility. The mechanically conceived universe of René Descartes, and all those which followed it to the end of the last century, were very different from the world in whose existence creative artists invite us to believe. Given a certain quantity of extended matter and the elementary laws of motion, Descartes could make bold to reconstruct a priori just such a universe as the one we live in. No artist ever lived in such a world. Not that there is less intelligibility in the universe of a modern painter than there was in the world of Descartes, but instead of preceding being, as

---

[10] See Eric Gill's letter to William Rothenstein, February 25, 1917 (in *Letters, op. cit.,* pp. 88f.) : "I am speaking only of the actual work—the paint or the stone—and not at all of its significance or meaning or value in the abstract, what it's 'worth to God,' but simply what it *is*. On the one side are e.g.: Giotto, etc.; Persian Rugs; Bricks & Iron Girders; Tools, Steam engines; Folk Song; Plain Song; Caligraphy [*sic*]; Toys (not some few modern ones tho.) ; Animals; Men & Women physically regarded; Hair; Lines; String; Plaited Straw; Beer & so on. On the other are Velázquez, Rembrandt, etc. No, this second list is too difficult—what I wish to convey is that such things as I name in the 1st. list & such things as young children's drawings & the works of savages are themselves actually a part of nature, organically one with nature and in no sense outside her—while, on the other hand, the work of Rembrandt & most moderns (the modern contribution—the renaissance) is not a part of nature but is apart from nature—is in fact an appreciation & a criticism of nature—a reviewing of nature as of something to be loved or hated. Good criticism is an excellent thing—why not? Well, it's no good trying to write all this—I wish we could meet & thrash it out." We intentionally preserve these last lines, as a symbol of the discouragement artists experience when they try to talk about art. Cf. the letter to Walter Shewring, March 28, 1933 (pp. 275f.), and to *The Friend,* July 14, 1933 (p. 277), where Gill forcibly restates his distinction between in-terpretative art and creative art—that is, "between the works which 'hold a mirror up to nature' and those which are themselves *part* of nature. It is clear that the characteristic works of post-Renaissance painters and sculptors are of the interpretative kind, while the works of the European and Indian middle ages and those of China, Mexico, Egypt and all 'primitive' and 'savage' peoples are of the other kind. They are 'natural' objects in the sense that they are the natural product of the kind of being that man is—a creature that needs things for use, who delights in making what he needs and who can only with difficulty be prevented from making things in such a way as that they please him when made."—Cf. George Braque, *Le Jour et la nuit* (Paris: Gallimard, 1952) p. 13: "The painter does not strive to reconstitute an anecdote, but to constitute a pictorial fact."

it naturally does in a world for knowledge, intelligibility attends it and finds in it its very foundation in the world of intelligible qualities familiar to creative artists. It is a universe that is always trying to say more than has already been said, or, at least, to say it otherwise; but it does not yet know the sense of what it is about to say; the sense will be clear as soon as the words are found to say it. Yet there is surely going to be a sense; otherwise there would be no words. So also with paintings. All significant works of art, however much they may at first surprise the eye, the ear, or the mind, ultimately reveal the inner intelligibility without which they would not *be*. But it is in giving being to their works that painters themselves realize their intelligibility.

However we may interpret them—and artists are not responsible for the reflections inspired by their art—the facts on which these remarks are founded should remain present in our mind, be it only as so many invitations to pursue the dialogue with the discoveries of modern art as eagerly as we do with the discoveries of modern science. It would be difficult to say which ones are the more important, not indeed in the order of practical life, where applied science reigns supreme, but in the disinterested order of philosophical speculation. A lifetime is not too long to understand the message of so many paintings waiting for us everywhere on the surface of the earth, but one cannot begin too soon to listen to what it says. Nor should one be afraid to embark on the somewhat strange adventures to which we are invited by some of these masterpieces. It is only too possible that some of them will always remain for us like those secret domains of which, in dreams, we vainly try to find the key. In such cases, we shall never know who was at fault, but the odds are on genius. He who sincerely exposes himself to creative art and agrees to share in its ventures will often be rewarded by the discovery, made in joy, that an endlessly increasing accumulation of beauty is, even now, in progress on this man-inhabited planet. At a still higher level, he will know the exhilarating feeling of finding himself in contact with the closest analogue there is, in human experience, to the creative power from which all the beauties of art as well as those of nature ultimately proceed. Its name is Being.

NOVELTY, OTHERNESS

BERNARD BERENSON

When we have taken cognizance of the constituting elements of an object, so that for us with our training, our profession, and our prepared expectations there is nothing more to discover for the time being, that object begins to bore us. We sidle away from it, avoid it, and succeed in forgetting it; unless indeed, as happens to many when young or perpetuated in adolescence, we insult over the corpse of our dead but not yet buried admiration. We thereupon begin to hanker for a fresh object upon which to exercise our cognitive faculties, a state of mind which can best be described as a lust for novelty, for otherness. It is a lust that has greater power in art than in life itself, art being so much more plastic, more ductile, more fluid than life.

Novelty, otherness, then consists in the easy, but not too easy, satisfaction given to the cognitive faculties when these throw themselves upon

From Aesthetics and History in the Visual Arts. *Copyright 1948 by Pantheon Books, Inc. Reprinted by permission of Pantheon Books, Inc.*

an object after exhausting a prior one. It is so full of craving, so lustful that it is no better judge of the artistic qualities of the object procuring this satisfaction than the physiological or chemical affection known as being-in-love is a judge of the moral character of its object. And just as love cannot assert itself, and make sure of its reality, until being-in-love is over, so artistic qualities can be descried only when the excitement and fever of newness has cooled. Few are gifted by nature, and not all of these have the education and training to extricate themselves from the metaphysics, philosophies, misinformations, and prejudices (sucked up in their preconscious, earliest years) that beset the approach to the work of art, if it is. to be enjoyed for its intrinsic qualities and not for its newness. Moreover, it requires intelligent cooperation. We cannot remain passive. We must be not only receptive, but responsive.

They who can enjoy and feel in the artifact little more than its otherness, its novelty, are like nomads who quickly use up a territory and dash on in search of new game, in quest of fresh pasturage, or, if they are already consumers of cereals, in the hope of soil still untouched, to skim in passing. The nomads in the realm of art would leave no more trace of their excitement and exhilaration than have the migrants of old.

If it were fashion alone of which people wearied—fashion begotten by the love of novelty or the lust for showing off—the loss would be small. They, however, who enjoy little in the artifact except its novelty will get as weary of what in the work of art is of more than passing interest and is of enduring value. They will laugh and jeer at masterpieces that they have done with, as they will run down last year's extravagances. Thus generations and centuries may pass before a Botticelli is rediscovered or, still later and more tumultuously, a Piero della Francesca. Brought to notice again, along with the glorious company of their contemporaries, they do their stunt as at a variety show, are applauded, called back again and again, and then forgotten in favor of some other exhumation of the past, more poignantly novel because more and more remote from our traditional standards. So we Atlantic peoples have reduced the Quattrocento to a single artist, Piero della Francesca, as the Central Europeans have narrowed down the Cinquecento to Michelangelo, while the most advanced of us turn up our noses at all of these and find no satisfaction for our exquisite cravings except in the frescoes of Mount Athos, in pre-Cimabue Madonnas, in the incunabulae of Romanesque sculpture, in Negro wood-carvings, South Sea idols, and Tlinkit totem-poles.

The lust for otherness, for newness, which seems the most natural and matter-of-course thing in the world, is neither ancient nor universal. Prehistoric races are credited with having had so little of it that a change in artifacts is assumed to be a change in populations, one following another. The same holds for the more or less unhistorical peoples of relatively recent or quite recent date like the Peruvians and the Mayas and Aztecs as well as the African and Oceanic tribes. Even people so civilized as the Egyptians changed so little in three thousand years that it takes training to distinguish a Saitic sculpture from one of the early dynasties. In Mesopotamia also change was slow. But for Alexander's conquest there might have been almost no newness in India, and but for the Buddhist missionaries as little in China. Why was there so little craving for novelty everywhere on the earth? It could scarcely have been due to the possibility that the sources of visual pleasure, stored up in extant artifacts, were so inexhaustible that no demand for new ones could arise. Likely enough people were too inert, too indolent to use their cognitive faculties, and crave for change. It would seem as if the Greeks were responsible for the introduction of this hankering for otherness, for newness, with a spirit so opposed to the ancient Egyptians and Persians that the priests of the one and the satraps of the other could compare them to unruly children. The Greeks carried this spirit with them wherever they went, but without permanent effects upon Asiatics and Africans, who tended to stay where they were to mummify and ossify like Copts or Mesopotamians, Arabs or Hindus, with almost no conscious need of newness, with no liability to change, excepting of course under such destructive or creative impact from the outside as came to India with the Greeks after Alexander, with the Arabs after Mohammed, and with Turkish tribes in late medieval Persia. The West, on the other hand, was entirely won over to the spirit of change. Our most stagnant moments have been of a relatively short duration, and not devoid of stirrings; while from the beginning of the present millennium change has been continuous and ever quicker. Finally in this twentieth century it is conquering the entire earth. Before long we shall have to voyage to the shores of western Kamchatka in search of the last unchanging folkways and artifacts, to be disappointed perhaps when we got there.

In protohistoric times, then, change occurred only when there was a displacement of population, tribes succeeding tribes, bringing their own artifacts. In prehistory such clean sweeps must have been even rarer. Occupation of the land had become too complete and too dense for massacre or pestilence to leave it empty for newcomers. If these arrived

as conquerors they killed some of the best artificers with as little awareness or conscience as had the Roman legionary who cut down Archimedes at Syracuse. Others they enslaved and compelled to cater to their
own nomadic and infantile tastes. As a rule the ancient occupants ended
by getting the upper hand of the invaders, and were perhaps the better
for the enrichment received from the fresh blood the newcomers poured
into the veins of their common descendants.

CREATIVE ART,

WORK, AND PLAY

C. J. DUCASSE

Play may, I think, accurately be characterized as *the systematic pursuit of an end set up or accepted expressly for the purpose.*[1] The end which is ostensibly pursued in play, is in fact only a means to, or precondition of, the pursuing activities which constitute the play. The immediate enjoyment of these (which is not necessarily due to expenditure of surplus energy) is the true "end" of play, i.e., it is the answer to the reflective question, Why do it? Play is thus *activity, telic in form only, performed for its own sake.* Taken in this sense, the characterization of it as *autotelic* activity is correct. It is to be noted, incidentally, that the question whether an end which is being pursued is really wanted, or is only a pretext for the pleasure of pursuing it, is one which can be an-

From The Philosophy of Art (*New York: The Dial Press, Inc., 1929*). Reprinted by permission of the author.

[1] As will be noticed, the well-known facetious definition of philosophy as the systematic abuse of an elaborate technical terminology invented expressly for the purpose has for its very effect the exhibiting of philosophy *as mere play.*

swered by the spectator as well as by the performer. Thus an activity may be play from the standpoint of the one, and not from that of the other; and we find adults calling play some activities of children about which the children themselves are in deadly earnest, and which they would not class with the activities that *they* call play. . . .

Although art, like play, differs from work in not being a means to an end external to itself, there is yet between art and play this great difference (and between art and work this likeness), namely, that art is essentially productive, creative; while play is not. Hirn, who clearly perceives this, writes:[2] "The aim of play is attained when the surplus of vigor is discharged or the instinct has had its momentary exercise. But the function of art is not confined to the act of production; in every manifestation of art, properly so called, something is made and something survives. . . ."[3]

PLAY IS AUTOTELIC, WORK ECTOTELIC, AND ART ENDOTELIC

Groos' theory of play is obviously more adequate than the Schiller-Spencer theory, or the imitation and recreation theories, and it is, I think, sound in essentials. But it does not seem to me that Groos has succeeded any better than Spencer in showing that art is to be regarded as the *play* of the higher faculties.

If, biologically considered, play is what Groos maintains, namely, the agency through which crude powers are developed and prepared for life's uses, then it seems impossible to regard either artistic production or aesthetic contemplation as play. No one would maintain that the art of singing, for instance, is a playful exercise of the voice, preparing it to be used perhaps in calling for help more loudly when dangers arise; and in the case of most other arts—piano or violin playing, for instance, or painting—it would be still more difficult to suggest even such an absurdly far-fetched biological utility to either the performer or his public. The most plausible instance that could be adduced of an art closely similar in externals to an activity that constitutes play as biologically defined by Groos, would probably be the art of acting; and the capacity to act a part does have biological and social utility in deceiving enemies, rivals, or prey. Yet no one could seriously maintain that what

---

[2] *The Origins of Art* (New York: The Macmillan Company, 1900), p. 29.

[3] The view of play implicit in the above quotation is, however, not here endorsed.

the actor, or the novelist, or in general the practitioner of a representative art, is engaged in, can be described as the developing and preparing for life's uses, of his crude natural powers of lying! Thus, art is not biologically, like play, practice or rehearsal of anything. Moreover, art-production, and aesthetic contemplation, are, like work, serious activities, while play and amusements are not, but only at times intent and absorbing. Again, as already mentioned, art is essentially creative, while play is not; and the experimentation which Groos mentions as present in all creative activity is not, as he terms it, playful, but on the contrary earnest. It is enjoyed, but is not engaged in with the view of enjoying oneself, as games are. It is engaged in for the sake of creating something, i.e., it has an end, and the creating of it is regarded as something that one *must* do—it is a real end, not, as in play, a trumpery one. The obligation to attain it, however, is not as in work external and conditional, but internal to art, and categorical. Art, as thus *containing* a real end, is not autotelic but *endotelic;* whereas work is properly termed *ectotelic* (or heterotelic). The obligation of art is a categorical imperative, uttered, as it were, to ourselves by ourselves. It is the obligation imposed by the laws of one's inward being, to give birth to that which one bears darkly in oneself. From play, however, this character of obligation is wholly absent. Playing chess, for instance, so long as it is play, could not be described as a means to the mating of the opponent's king; nor is any obligation to attempt it felt. Play, as already stated above, is only the enjoyed systematic pursuit of an end set up or accepted expressly for the purpose.[4]

Between art and work, moreover, there is also this difference: In work the particular nature of the end to which the work is (or is believed to be) the means, is clearly known beforehand. In art, on the contrary, the particular nature of that which one is in process of creating is clearly known only after it is created. Therefore, whereas work can be described as successful or unsuccessful in the sense that the product of it does or does not copy the particular antecedently conceived desired

---

[4] Cf. Henri Delacroix, *Psychologie de l'art* (Paris: F. Alcan, 1927). "The true difference [between play and art] is elsewhere. Play is almost indifferent to its material. It does not attempt to make of it anything beyond the momentary signification which it confers upon it. The player uses his playthings only as means to reach his ends, as symbols on which to hook up his intentions. The intrinsic nature of his objects matters little to him; it is enough that they be transfigured by the action and the theme of the play" (p. 44) ; and also: "Play has disclosed itself to us as an activity exercising itself outside the constraint of reality and which creates, according to the interests and the mental level of the player, the themes and the objects necessary to its exercise" (p. 42).

end; art, on the other hand, can be spoken of as successful or unsuccessful only in the different sense that its product is or is not such as to reimpart in contemplation the same subjective state from which it sprang, and of which that product is not at all a copy in a material denser than images, but an objectification, no matter whether in image or in sensation-material.[5] In other words, in work, what occurs is the creating of a real *object* copying a desired and merely imagined *object*. But in art what occurs is the creating of an object, whether real or imaginal, and of a nature not antecedently known, which in a unique way corresponds *to something that was not an object at all,* viz., to a feeling.

In bringing to an end these remarks with regard to the mutual relations of play, art, and work, it may further be noted with regard to play that, especially in the plays of youth, the biological function of play is doubtless what Gross asserts, namely, to prepare, educate, or develop the powers involved. But in other cases, such as many of the plays of adults, the biological function of play is rather to be thought of as the keeping from atrophy of powers already developed; and in other cases yet, as that of harmlessly sublimating surplus energy. This, however, does not necessarily imply (although it admits as a possibility more or less often realized) that in such cases the pressure of accumulated surplus energy itself occasions the play; nor does it imply that the surplus energy expanded was stored up in the particular organs used in the play. Fitness of a given organ to function, and surplus of energy in the organism as a whole, seem to be rather distinct things. It is worth noting also that it is not of the essence of play not to be directly productive of valuable external results. A useful activity in which one has attained considerable virtuosity may come to be engaged in independently of the fact that its result possesses utility. That is, it may be engaged in for the fun of it—with the mere pleasure of the performance as end—and thus be play, although useful. Thus, we hear it said that some expert surgeons at times remove appendixes for the pleasure of the operation, i.e., in play. Supposing this true, the possibility that the appendix in a given such case really needed to be removed, so that the surgeon's act in that case turned out to have a directly useful objective

---

[5] Croce correctly perceives that the copying in perceptual stuff of something already existing in image stuff is not art. His error, as it seems to me, is in not recognizing that art may and often does create as *directly* in perceptual stuff as in image stuff.

result, would not rob that act of its character of play from his standpoint.

Lastly, in addition to work, play, and art, mention must also be made of activities which are carried on automatically, and to which the teleological categories of means and end are inapplicable. Such activities may therefore be called *atelic*. Automatic activities are the reflex, instinctive, and habitual activities, such as swallowing, breathing, undressing, shifting one's position in a chair, scratching oneself, and many others. Such activities, when truly describable as automatic, take place without conscious attention either to them or to their results, and therefore cannot be characterized either as means or as ends, from the standpoint of the performer of them at the time. Automatic activities of some sorts may well, as Groos contends, be preliminary to play, but they themselves are not properly called play. . . .

ART IN GENERAL; ENDOTELIC ART; AESTHETIC ART

Art, in the broadest sense of the term, is activity which is consciously so controlled as to produce a result satisfying some specified condition. On the basis of the classification of telic activities made in the last chapter, we may divide art as so defined into *ectotelic* art (the utilitarian arts—skilled work, or engineering in the widest sense), *autotelic* art (skill in games and play), and *endotelic* art (skilled self-objectification), of which "art" in the most common sense of the term . . . is one species.

Endotelic art resembles play in that the end aimed at is not imposed from without, as in work, but is imposed by oneself. In play, however, the ostensible end which one adopts or sets to oneself is not really valued; its true status is that of a means to or condition of the pleasure of pursuit, which is what is really wanted or valued. Play is thus an activity, *telic in form only,* which is performed for its own sake. In this sense it may properly be called autotelic activity. Endotelic art differs from play in that the self-imposed end which it aims at is really wanted; it is not trumped up for the pleasure of pursuing it but is considered as something that *ought* to be achieved. In this respect, endotelic art resembles work; but it differs from work in that the "ought" of work is conditional, imposed from without, whereas the "ought" of endotelic art is categorical, imposed by the artist's own being; or, as we may therefore say, endotelic art is a free activity, and work as such, and directly, is not.

The end which endotelic art seeks, is objectification of the artist's self, i.e., of his feelings, meanings, or volitions. The art which is endotelic may then be said to consist in *conscious or critically controlled objectification of self;* or, equivalently, in *consciously objective self-expression.* Endotelic art then is of three sorts, according as what it seeks to objectify is feeling, meaning, or will. *Aesthetic art,* which is what usually is referred to when the word "Art" is used without qualification, is the conscious objectification of one's feelings. As distinguished from it, the conscious objectification of one's meanings, usually in words, may be called *lectical art;* and the conscious objectification of one's volitions, *heuretic art.* . . .

MEANING OF "OBJECTIFICATION."

The definition of endotelic art in general, given above, is highly compact, and, to make its meaning fully clear it is necessary to consider next some of the terms that enter into it. After that, we shall limit our discussion to the one species of endotelic art with which we are essentially concerned in these pages, namely, aesthetic art.

The first thing that needs to be made clear is the meaning attached in the definition of endotelic art to the words "Objectification," or "Objective Expression." They are not intended to imply that the feeling, meaning, or volition which is expressed is necessarily expressed in perceptual material, i.e., in material rendering observation by others than the artist possible. Objectification, indeed, is usually partially at least in perceptual stuff, but it might take place wholly in image-stuff, and thus remain private to the artist. The limitations of image-stuff as medium of expression have already been pointed out; they are empirical only. Theoretically, therefore, image-stuff is possible stuff for any expression. This is recalled at this point only to make clear that objectivity does not necessarily mean perceptual objectivity.

What is meant here by speaking of objectification, or of expression as objective, is that the act of expression is (in such a case) creative of something (1) capable of being contemplated by the artist at least, and (2) such that *in contemplation that thing yields back to him the feeling, meaning, or volition of which it was the attempted expression.* Thus, one would be said to have objectified or expressed objectively one's meaning if, in reading the words which one wrote, one obtains back from them the very meaning which one attempted to express, so that one is then able to say, "Yes, that is exactly what I meant." If on the contrary one finds oneself forced to say in reading or listening to one's own words: "No, this is not just what I meant," then one's attempt to objectify one's meaning has failed. Such an unsuccessful attempt constitutes expression only in the subjective sense of the term. That is, although it may rid us, at least for the time being, of the impulse to express our given meaning, it does not rid us of it by objectifying it. But as noted in an earlier chapter, unsuccessful attempts at objective self-expression cannot be distinguished from successful by the way they feel at the time, but only by contemplating their products and noting whether or not the latter mirror back to us accurately what we attempted to express. It should be noted, however, that this obtaining back from the object created, of what we tried to express, is *only the proof* of the success of the attempt at objective expression. It is not an end, other than objective self-expression, to which the object is intended as means and for the sake of which it is created. Or, if it is that, then our creative activity was essentially not endotelic art, but ectotelic, viz., skilled work, as when we construct a physical mirror to the end of examining ourselves.

However, even in cases where the attempt at objective self-expression is, upon contemplation of its product, judged to have been wholly successful, one might question whether the feeling, meaning, or volition reflected to us in such contemplation can be said to be truly *the same* as that which orginally we had to express. As to this, it must of course be admitted that something happens as a result of objectification. But what happens is not a change in the intrinsic nature—in the "what"—of the feeling, meaning, or volition; it is only a gain in the clearness or the steadiness with which we experience or live it. Unless qualitative identity were preserved in the process of clarification, . . . there would be nothing of which we could say that *it* has been clarified. Ever since the early days of Greek philosophy, it has been recognized that if anything is to be described as a change, and not as an outright substitution, something must remain identical through the process.

IN WHAT SENSE OBJECTIFICATION IS CONSCIOUS

Acts of self-expression are blind and irresponsible whenever they have not been rehearsed, that is to say, whenever the expression is of something original, new, not expressed before. Although one's every feeling, thought, or volition is somewhat like some other or others, yet it is usually also somewhat different from others, and to that extent new.

To that extent the expression of it is therefore blind. Such blind self-expression might nevertheless possess objectivity in the sense of that term specified above, but even then it would not yet constitute art, for it is of the essence of art to be not blind like automatic action, but conscious and responsible. That is, art is not merely self-expression, nor even merely objective self-expression, but *consciously* objective self-expression; its product must not only be capable of passing the test of objectivity described, but must have actually passed it. This means that art can objectify the new only by a process of "trial and error," or more accurately, of trial and criticism, and if need be, correction. There may very well be, and often there is, but a single trial, completely successful by itself. But whether there be but one, or more than one, every trial at the moment it occurs is itself blind as to whether or not it has achieved objectivity of expression. Consciousness of this has to be gained, and is gained immediately afterwards, by contemplation of the product of the trial, and critical judgment of it, i.e., judgment either that it does or does not, truly mirror back the inner state to which we wished to give expression. To say that the objective self-expression which is (endotelic) art, is conscious—or, which is the same thing, that the self-expression which is (endotelic) art is expression critically controlled in such manner as to achieve objectivity—therefore does not mean that it need be conscious or so controlled either antecedently to or contemporaneously with the expressive act. Only rehearsal would make this possible. But it does mean that *a critical judgment is an intrinsic, essential constituent of the productive activity called art;* and indeed, not merely a critical judgment, but a *favorable* one. That is to say, the art has failed—there has been not skill but rather blundering—unless one has not merely judged the product of one's activity in respect to its objectivity, but judged it actually to have attained to objectivity. One must be able to acknowledge the product as an adequate statement of oneself.

The activity in which a new feeling, meaning, or volition expresses itself proceeds from an impulse which at the moment is blind, and as such cannot strictly be said to be *aiming* at anything, but only manifesting itself. It is therefore only in terms of the later observation of the sort of product which it tends to have, that it is describable as impulse to self-objectification. Thus, the telic character, which truly belongs to art since a critical moment is an intrinsic part of it, may be said to accrue to the expressive activity which is its first moment, *ex post facto*. That activity is telically construed and criticized, *after* it has occurred. And the work of art is not the product of that activity simply, but of that activity telically construed and criticized, and if need be repeated until correction of the product results, i.e., until objectivity of the expression is obtained.

CORRECTION OF THE PRODUCT OF ATTEMPTED OBJECTIFICATION, VS. CORRECTION OF THE SELF FIRST OBJECTIFIED.

The process of correction (if any) which culminates in the acknowledgment of the product as adequate statement of oneself is, however, susceptible of two different interpretations. It may mean that the earlier attempt at objective self-expression was not completely successful; but it may also mean that it was a successful objectification of a self which, when it confronted us clearly, we disowned and repudiated in favor of another, namely, of the self which found adequate objectification in the "corrected" product—the product being then better describable as objectification of a corrected self. . . .

IN WHAT SENSE ULTERIOR ENDS MAY COEXIST WITH ENDOTELIC ART-CREATION.

The endotelic character of the activity which has been described as conscious objectification of self, involves, as we have seen, that it is a free or autonomous activity. This autonomy of endotelic art does not, however, exclude the possibility that ulterior purposes should be at the same time served by it. What it forbids is that such ulterior purposes should govern, or even have any voice in, the critical process mentioned above as constituting an intrinsic part of art-creation. The fact is often brought forward that many lyrical poems, for instance, have actually been composed to win the favor of a lady. One may, however, seek to win the favor of a lady by revealing to her one's inmost self, such as it may be; or, on the other hand, by displaying to her such a self as one thinks she will like, pretending it to be one's own.

In the first case, the composing of the poem that bares one's soul is (aesthetic) art. It is an autonomous activity, in the sense that the only consideration in the light of which the critical process involved is exercised is that of the adequacy with which what was done objectifies *oneself*. That is, such corrections as may be made, are made not so that the product may objectify something more adequate to the end of winning the lady, but so that it may more adequately objectify that which is *oneself*. The burden of winning the lady is left to the nature and quality of that self, such as it is; and the concern of art in the whole affair is only to reveal it truly. The art-activity even here determines and contains within itself its own end, and is responsible only to itself. Such ulterior purposes as its product may then be turned to, remain irrelevant to that activity. The man as a whole may have such ulterior purposes, but the man as artist has not.

In the second case, on the other hand, where verses are written displaying whatever sort of self one thinks the lady will like—which self one passes off as one's own—what we have is not aesthetic nor even endotelic art at all. It is only beautiful lying skilfully adapted to the end of seduction. It is angling with spiritual bait, amatory engineering, i.e., an instance of ectotelic art, skilled work. . . .

THE DEFINITION OF AESTHETIC ART PROPOSED DIFFERENTIATES IT FROM CASES OF EXPRESSION WHICH ARE NOT ART; AND ALSO FROM SKILLED WORK.

From this point on, we shall be concerned only with aesthetic art, and we may therefore agree, for convenience and in conformity with ordinary usage, to employ simply the word "Art" whenever aesthetic art is meant, unless special notice is given that this convention is for the time being departed from. . . .

Here it remains to show that the definition of (aesthetic) art proposed does apply to whatever is acknowledgedly so called, and at the same time excludes various things which in spite of certain likenesses to art nevertheless are not art. It may be pointed out in the first place that the definition given distinguishes expressions of feeling which are art from those which, like yawning, laughing, stretching, etc., are not art. The character which truly distinguishes art from such other expressions of feeling is the critical control in respect to objectivity, which is an intrinsic part of art; and not (for reasons already stated) the deliberate intention to infect others with feeling, proposed as specific difference by Tolstoi. As to Croce's proposed *differentia* for the expression which is art, viz., being "aesthetic" as distinguished from "naturalistic," it is useless because virtually but verbal. That is, it does little except give a name to the distinction sought, since the terms "spiritual" and "active" by which he further describes the sort of expression which is "aesthetic" are themselves left far too ambiguous and vague to separate clearly the "aesthetic" sheep of expression from its "naturalistic" goats.

Critical control, again, is what distinguishes art from expressions of feeling which achieve objectivity but do so unconsciously. There are probably, for instance, cases where a feeling is expressed spontaneously and naturally in an action, and where the action at the same time happens to constitute as objective an expression of the feeling as it could if it were not action but acting. However, because no critical control is involved in such cases, they do not constitute art. Still farther, of course, are we from having art in the much more numerous cases where the spontaneous, natural expression of feeling does not have objectivity as defined above.

It is to be noted also that a work of art would not be sufficiently characterized as an artificial thing embodying a feeling. That the creative process shall be critically controlled *in the particular manner described,* viz., so that it shall exactly objectify the creator's feeling, is a specification necessary to rule out processes by which an object embodying a feeling is created, but which do not constitute art. An instance of such would be the technical processes of color-photography, printing, and so on, by which are produced accurate copies of original paintings. The critical control involved in such processes is directed not as in aesthetic art to the end that the thing created shall adequately objectify the creator's feeling, but to the end that it shall discharge as effectively as possible the function of substitute for an already existing object, namely, the original. If the copy is faithful, it will indeed constitute an embodiment of the same feeling as the original; but the process which brought the copy into existence is nevertheless not to be called aesthetic art, for it does not constitute an attempt by the performer to objectify a feeling present in himself. He is not expressing a feeling but copying an object, whether mechanically or otherwise; and he need never have himself so much as experienced the feeling which is objective in the product of his work. What we have in such a case is only skilled work—ectotelic art. . . .

THE FEELING WHICH AN ELABORATE WORK OF ART FINALLY OBJECTIFIES IS NOT USUALLY PRESENT *AB INITIO;* BUT DEVELOPS STEP BY STEP.

There is another matter concerning which misunderstanding might arise when a work of art is characterized as the objective expression of a feeling. This might be taken to imply that the rich and highly determinate feeling which contemplation of an elaborate completed work of art reveals as embodied therein was present in its fullness from the very outset in the artist. But as already pointed out, the presence there *ab initio* of the feeling that the work finally objectifies is on the contrary likely to be a fact only in simple, elementary expressions of feeling. The usual state of affairs is rather that the feeling which the work of art finally comes to embody is born in the artist only gradually, its growth preceding by but little the process of its objectification. What generally is present in the artist at the outset is a feeling which, in its relation to the feeling which the finished elaborate work will embody, may be characterized both as germinal and as general. It is the *germ* out of which gradually grows the feeling finally embodied—the steps in its growth following contemplation of the object already created at any given moment. The original feeling is at the same time *general* in the sense that it provides a test of the relevance of the multifarious other feelings which, as the artist works, crowd into his consciousness and clamor for expression; the original feeling thus being, in relation to the later ones, analogous in function to a framework or rough sketch, into which the later must either fit or be ruled out. As already insisted upon in an earlier passage where this step-by-step process was described, it does not essentially belong to the nature of the art-creative activity. It only constitutes the history of the psychological genesis of the feeling which certain works of art (viz., complicated, elaborate ones), objectify when they are called finished. The art-creative act, whether it be one of a series or not, and whether it be itself performed not at one stroke but in several (i.e., with correcting strokes), nevertheless always consists in an attempt to express objectively such feeling as exists at the time; and the act is complete when this is judged to have been done adequately.

There are exceptional cases on record, where, in highly gifted artists, even the feeling which a completed elaborate work of art objectifies appears to have been present in its fullness and vigor at the very start. For instance there is the case referred to by Stewart,[6] of a girl, a talented musician, who speaks of an "absolute music," "music in her head," "music with a sound which she cannot quite hear," music which it often "annoys her to have to embody (so imperfectly!) in the actual sounds of voice or instrument." Or again, the case of Mozart: "The piece, he tells us, came to him as a whole, often in bed, or when he was walking. It articulated itself in his head, till he 'heard' it, not as a succession of sounds, but, as it were, 'all together'" (p. 153). This, so

---

[6] *Plato's Doctrine of Ideas* (Oxford: The Clarendon Press, 1909), pp. 152ff.

far as the description permits of judging, might be either the feeling that the piece as a whole embodies as eventually played; or else perhaps an adequate objectification of that feeling purely in imagined terms, and of which the actual playing would then be in this particular case for Mozart, mere copying.

NATURALISM

AND CREATIVITY

ELISEO VIVAS

Contemporary naturalists urge the acceptance of their philosophy on the ground that it is not open to the criticism that led to the discrediting of the materialistic philosophy of the Nineteenth century from which it descends. Claiming to be more sympathetic to the demands of the contemporary world than traditional philosophers, as they frequently remind us (as if sympathy for such a world were something for which one could take credit) these thinkers believe that they are able to avoid the facile techniques of reductionistic analysis of the older naturalism; and thus, they argue, they are able to do full justice to the higher values of religion, morality, and art. As J. H. Randall, Jr. puts it, naturalism "is not only not unsympathetic to the genuine values on which anti-naturalists have insisted. It is convinced that it feels them as strongly

From Creation and Discovery (*New York: The Noonday Press, 1955*). *Reprinted, with corrections, by permission of the author.*

and understands them better than their protagonists." [1] In the following pages one naturalistic theory of mind will be examined—that presented by Y. H. Krikorian in the book in which Mr. Randall makes this assertion. The examination shows that Mr. Randall's claim cannot be accepted, because Mr. Krikorian's theory neglects important data which it is necessary to reckon with in order to do justice to the workings of the human mind. If the criticism is valid, it invalidates, in an important sense, the kind of naturalism defended in the volume to which Mr. Krikorian makes his contribution. Kindly observe, however, that the results of the criticism do not allow for the unrestricted conclusion that all naturalism is therefore invalid. If another naturalistic theory of mind can account for these data, in that respect and to that extent a naturalistic philosophy is possible. Naturalism, however, does not succeed, when its proponents exhort us to employ the scientific method and promise us that if we do we shall solve all our problems. A philosophy cannot base its claims to validity on promissory notes.

Krikorian's view of mind is behavioristic, he tells us, because "behavior is the only aspect of mind which is open to experimental examination." [2] Unfortunately the reader runs immediately into difficulty, because Krikorian forgets to tell him what the naturalist does about those aspects of mind which are not open to the behavioristic approach. That there are such aspects is clearly implied by his statement, but we need not be informed of them by the author to know that they exist. There are, for instance, the purely private aspects of experience—the immediately felt quality of our affective life. This aspect of mind is incommunicable, yet of its importance there is no doubt, since it includes not only the felt quality of mere sense experience but a wide range of affective aspects which determine decisively our valuational attitudes. There are also those submerged processes of the psyche which we dimly envisage by tortuously roundabout and fleeting means of a purely introspective, nonbehavioral nature: the field, I mean, which psychoanalysis has preempted. And there are finally the "creative" activities which take place beyond the range of experimental examination and through which men

---

[1] *Naturalism and the Human Spirit*, Yervant H. Krikorian, ed. (New York: Columbia University Press, 1944), p. 381. This volume will be referred to hereafter as *Naturalism*. It is advisable to note "for the record" that the author of this note is one of the contributors to *Naturalism*. But if he once called himself a naturalist, the reader of his contribution to his book will notice, as one of the philosophers who reviewed it noticed, that even when he accepted the label, he was far from sharing the temper of the naturalist philosophy as represented by the majority of his fellow contributors.

[2] *Ibid.* p. 252.

somehow transform their experience—in the fields of science, art, morality, religion, and industry—and, as it seems, add something to it which was not there before.

The decision to use only data that can be brought under experimental examination gives rise to the question whether the philosopher can both neglect the nonbehavioral aspects of mind and at the same time offer a complete and adequate theory of mind. If this question is answered with a reply to the effect that the naturalist is better off if he stays within the area of the positively known, we reply that he cannot both claim that he understands better than his opponent those genuine values on which the latter has insisted and at the same time admit limitations of method that block such understanding. A scientist can narrow his inquiry down to such subject matter as his method can properly handle, for he passes no judgment on what falls outside his purview; but a philosopher does not have the same privilege, for he not only sets himself out, as Krikorian puts it, "to understand mind," but he must attempt to give us a comprehensive account of human values and a plausible theory of human destiny. This, his main task, is a pressing one that does not await that remote and glorious day when science shall have found out everything there is to find about the mind. One often hears naturalists, particularly positivists, repudiate the role that I have assigned to philosophy on the ground that the problem of human destiny is a meaningless problem. The answer is that you cannot avoid it by denying it or ignoring it; for all you do in that case is to refuse to face it critically, and instead of an explicit conception open to rational correction you accept uncritically the philistine notion of destiny which is implicit in the organization of values (such as it is) of the day and world in which you live.

While Krikorian claims that on behavioral terms he is able to "understand mind," I doubt if there are many scientists who have looked into the problem of the creative imagination who are as daring as our scientistic philosopher in their boasts. The late Clark Hull, a leading behaviorist who earned his reputation in the laboratory, was under no illusion that he knew enough to be able to give a scientific account of "the highest rational and moral behavior." [3] R. W. Gerard, a physiologist, approaching the problem of the imagination from the standpoint of his own interests, but, unlike Krikorian and Hull, willing to learn from psychoanalysts as well as from rigorous behaviorists, tells us that:

---

[3] Clark L. Hull, "Mind, Mechanism, and Adaptive Behavior," *Psychological Review*, Vol. XLIV, No. 1 (1934), 32ff.

It remains sadly true that most of our present understanding of mind would remain as valid and useful if, for all we knew, the cranium were stuffed with cotton wadding. In time, the detailed correlation of psychic phenomena and neural processes will surely come; but today we are hardly beyond the stage of unequivocal evidence that the correlation does exist.[4]

In spite of the way in which he prudently qualifies his statement, Gerard seems to be as full as Hull of generous unscientific faith that psychology and biology will some day overcome their limitations. And I, for my part, do not in the least doubt that if we are seeking nothing further than psychophysical correlations, we shall get them in increasing numbers in the future. That is not what Krikorian and Hull have as final aims; what they want to do is of course to get rid of the category of mind altogether. Whether the correlations that Gerard seeks will tell us all that, as humanists, we need to know about the creative process, is another matter. In the meantime it is only fair to wait for them before passing on their value, remarking in anticipation that until scientists are able to predict by observation of the nervous system or any other part of the body, and of the environment, whether a man is capable of writing an Inferno or an Oedipus Rex, and what the value, moral and aesthetic, of such work will be, the faith of our scientists about the importance of the light which their science can throw on the creative process is only of biographical interest and quite immaterial to our argument.

Since Krikorian may reply that this criticism is external and based on authority and that it makes too much of an unimportant sentence in his essay (that, namely, in which by implication he allowed that there were aspects of mind that the behavioral method could not handle), we must turn to the theory itself, although it will demand that we go into matters of a somewhat technical nature, and ask what explanation Krikorian offers of the creative activity.

Careful search does not reveal that this problem has been investigated by our author. But he no doubt considers that he has adequately handled it in the passages in which he gives us a theory of "reasoning or problem solving." We must therefore turn to this part of his essay to see if it satisfies our demands. Reasoning, which is to say, purposive thought, we are told, is

an anticipatory schema, a frame to be filled in. . . . The specific ideas that fill the schema are also anticipatory. Ideas are antici-

---

[4] R. W. Gerard, "The Biological Basis of Imagination," *The Scientific Monthly*, Vol. LXII (1946), 487.

pated operations and their consequences in relation to some situation. In behavioral terms, to have an idea is to be ready to respond in a specific way to a stimulus; to reason is to rehearse various anticipatory responses in relation to a problem. The difference, therefore, between reasoning and actual manipulation is that in the former case the operations are preseen and are only possible ones. When one says that one has an idea as to how a certain machine will work, one anticipates the series of operations which one would actually perform were one running the machine.[5]

Krikorian goes on to tell us that as ideas develop "they become more and more general in their application and abstract in their nature," freeing themselves gradually from specific operations and being performed by symbols. But he insists that "in this whole development of ideas anticipatory operations are basic." The process, however, through which ideas become abstract, and the manner in which symbols come to substitute for operations which in their basic reference remain nevertheless operational, are matters which are not gone into, although the reader suspects that this is one of the points on which strong evidence of a behavioral nature should be brought to bear and which requires the most rigorous analysis; for it is one of the points at which the antinaturalists have insisted that a break occurs in the natural process. Again, I doubt whether in order to have an idea of how a certain machine works one must rehearse anticipatorily operations performed when actually running the machine; for on this basis it would be difficult to explain how a teacher is able to teach, say, a musical instrument, although he himself cannot play it. Be that as it may, the problem to which we must confine ourselves is whether Krikorian can throw any light on what Coleridge called "the active imagination."

Krikorian holds that the anticipatory responses that constitute cognition or purposive thought "were previously experienced as actual consequences of the same kind of stimulus." But this constitutes a virtual denial of the possibility of creative increment. That this is not a mere slip of the pen on Krikorian's part is shown by the fact that elsewhere in the essay he tells us that "a physicist in his experimental work is guided by future results involved in his experiments; and a physician in making a presciption is controlled by the expected consequences of his medicine." This is unquestionably true of the physician in writing the ordinary prescription; but it is not true of the research men in medicine, nor is it true of the physicist.

The two cases of physician and physicist are mentioned by Krikorian

---

[5] *Naturalism, op. cit.,* p. 257.

at a point where he is interested in emphasizing the futuristic aspect of thought; but they do not illustrate the same type of "prospective cognition," and the failure anywhere throughout his discussion to mark the difference between them gives our author away. For it is to be hoped that the physician already has identified the nature of the disease for which he is prescribing and that he knows with reasonable certainty the effects of the medicine before he prescribes it. If he does not, he is irresponsible and of no interest to us in this discussion. The physicist may be merely checking an experiment that has already been performed, as a cook does in the kitchen who is not too certain of her art and is therefore trying to follow literally the directions of her Fannie Farmer. But as a creative mind, in first conceiving the experiment and in formulating the hypothesis which it is designed to test, the physicist has taken a leap beyond the already known and the already experienced. The same kind of leap of course is taken by the medical man when he gets a creative hunch. Krikorian tells us that we need not "make a mystery of the potentiality in the future reference of mind. The future possible consequences were previously experienced as actual consquences of the same kind of stimulus and were recorded in the neuromuscular system as 'neurograms.' "

It is interesting to note in passing that Krikorian, who insists on observable behavioral data subject to experimental control, has no scruples in falling back, when he thinks he needs them, on nonobservable entities called "neurograms" for the existence of which he does not offer the slightest evidence. Let us waive this point, however, and note the fact that the sentence which follows the quotation clearly indicates that he does not have in mind genuinely creative activity but that he is thinking of "problem-solving" at a very rudimentary level; for he says, "Thus, having been conditioned to the stimulus, they are ready to be set off by it when it is met again."

Krikorian is right in emphasizing the anticipatory aspect of thought. Mind is indeed, as he points out, prospective or futuristic; but unfortunately for his theory it is not so in the manner in which he tells us that it is. For thought is controlled, not only by "future consequences of stimuli which function as present stimuli," but teleologically, in a way that Krikorian does not seem to realize. To put it concretely, the thought of the physicist is controlled by a vague and inchoate whole, although at the moment of creative thinking he does not exactly know what that whole is. The new conception of the creative mind seems to come to birth under the guidance of an inchoate structure of ideas for which, since they have not yet been created, there can be as yet no "neurograms." If they were already recorded as neurograms, proof should be furnished of their presence, as well as of the fact that they are indeed consequences of stimuli previously experienced, for precisely what is at issue is this point, which on Mr. Krikorian's theory is settled by assertion.

Because I am less ignorant of aesthetics than I am of physics I am going to discuss the problem in terms of art rather than science; but the change should make no difference in the result, since it seems safe to assume that, viewed psychologically, the creative acts of both the physicist and of the artist are very similar. Now in art, what the behaviorist has to explain is the control that the new whole, which from the standpoint of consciousness has not yet been fully born, exercises over the artist's mind as he proceeds to bring it to birth. Mysteries are not elucidated by encouraging us not to recognize them as mysteries, and the creative act remains a mystery for the behaviorist in spite of his scientific courage and precisely because, by introducing his neurograms and his anticipatory expectations, he reduces the creative activity to a complex process of shuffling the already experienced. But for all its appearance of contemporaneity, this does not advance the theory of mind beyond the point where Hobbes left it. In order to make a significant advance the behaviorist would have to be able to account in his terms for the intentional mental direction, the purposive thrust of the mind, the mind's ability to follow the lead of something which is not pushing it from behind, so to speak, since it is not yet there. It is this fact, the control by the not-yet-there total situation over the present, that leads the idealist to insist that a factor is here at work of an essentially teleological nature; and until this factor is explained in its own terms and not by reduction (by implication) to simple problem-solving, according to which creative thinking consists in shuffling "neurograms" which were already formed, mind will continue to escape the efforts to bring it into line with behavioristic psychology.

A related difficulty which the behaviorist must face arises from the fact that the creative activity is not observable by behavioral techniques, nor even by close introspection. Consider for instance the celebrated case of Poincaré's successful research into Fuchsian functions.[6] The fact of which this case is an instance is itself very commonplace; if we discount Poincaré's stature and the importance of his discovery, we can say that

[6] H. Poincaré, *The Foundations of Science*, G. G. Halsted, trans. (New York: The Science Press, 1921), pp. 383 ff.

there is hardly any one who has not had the somewhat similar experience of solving a problem or elucidating a puzzle overnight. But how can we apply a theory of behaviorally observable anticipatory responses to the long unconscious work and the sudden illumination of which Poincaré gives us an account? Since for the behaviorist there is no consciousness, nothing can take place below its level. And yet somehow deep beyond the reach of observable behavior the creative mind transforms and transmutes the matter of experience, so that what it produces is in an important sense utterly unlike what was taken in by experience.

If this fact is denied, the burden of proof is on him who refuses to admit it as valid, and the proof would consist in showing that what we take to be new is not truly but only apparently new. In respect both to form and content the mind out of its own intrinsic spontaneity makes additions to its experience in the fields of science, art, statesmanship, morality, and religion. Nor is it possible to dissolve the difficulty by denying the validity of the distinction between form and content, for even if the denial were to be admitted, the problem would remain as to the source of the newness of the created object as a whole in respect to which no discrimination of structure as distinct from matter was admissible. The medium through which the addition is made—the language of the scientist or the material of the artist—resists, for it has obdurate ways over which the creative mind must win. But as the creative idea suddenly illumines consciousness, or slowly comes to birth, the matter yields and grows and is informed with something utterly new.

We know, of course, something about the observable aspects of the creative act—but what we know is superficial and trivial compared with what we do not know. It is not an exaggeration to say that in respect to its hidden factors we know nothing about the creative process, except that it does occur, and chiefly of course because the active imagination performs the synthesis of the old and brings about the creation of its new product unobserved, in the depths of the unconscious, if you will, after conscious effort gives it its first push. That in some minds the idea seems to pop fully formed and quite unexpectedly into consciousness, while in other no less gifted minds it has to be dragged out painfully piece by piece, and has to be fitted no less laboriously into completed wholes—these are all easily observable commonplaces. In the latter case, which is probably more common, it is easier to sense the effect of the not-yet-born whole controlling the process of creation, but that does not mean that in the former it was absent.

If the whole is there, in the depths of the unconscious, behaviorism will have to rescind its claims and the psychologist will have to give us an account of the manner in which the synthesis came about. The problem does not consist of the tracing of the old elements and distinguishing them as such, but of discovering the origin of the new, or of the disposal of the claim that anything new came into being. It is in respect to this puzzle that we seem to be utterly in the dark as to how the creative imagination goes about its work. Yet our ignorance is not so abysmal that it will allow us to confuse "the active imagination" with the capacity to solve problems evinced by the merely ingenious, the merely inventive mind. The difference may be only one of degree, though that is on the face of it doubtful; but a few degrees more or less mark an important difference in kind between the quick and the dead in body and may mark the difference between the mind of the genius and the merely ingenious mind.

It is true that we speak of the solution of problems on the part of both the creative scientist and the artist. Of the former it may be proper to speak in this manner, although there are reasons to doubt it. But of the artist, in spite of the fact that the expression is used idiomatically, it is not proper, and the acceptance of the phrase uncritically is likely to mislead us as to the actual process to which it refers. For only in a very qualified sense does the artist have before him a "problem" whose solution can be verified in terms of conditions objectively set *before* the "solution" is proposed. In the process of artistic creation the formulation of the conception and the solution of the problem are, I suspect, identical, and the creative process consists at once in creating and discovering what one wants to say. If the object thus "discovered" or "created" is a genuine product of art, it is as strange and fascinatingly new and unexpected to the artist when he finally brings it forth as it is to a competent audience. The activity of the artist has these two aspects —contradictory though they may seem—because the product presents itself to the artist, as he gradually "hits it off," as having an objective existence which controls the artist's activity and which resists his control, and yet as being, at the same time, the product of subjective propulsions and tensions that the artist can recognize as his own.

Perhaps the reason that we so readily talk about solving an artistic problem is the fact, already noted, that the for-consciousness-not-yet-there whole somehow tyrannizes over the artist, dictating what is admissible and what is not. However, although in ordinary discourse the phrase is not objectionable, when we are seeking the best light we can get on mental activity the expression can be a source of confusion. There are indeed difficulties that the artist can overcome and which, with little danger of confusion, may be spoken of as "problems," in the sense that the artist knows what he wants before he has found the way to achieve it. Such "problems" present themselves in regard to the manipulation of the medium when the artist feels that he has not yet come close enough to effects he clearly wants to achieve because he has clearly imagined them, but has not succeeded in quite hitting them off, or when he has to judge of the adequacy of a given form to a subject matter not yet informed that has begun to take shape in his mind. This is the case, for instance, when a poet thinks he can say what he wants in a sonnet and it turns out that a different "form" is required, or when he attempts a drama and after much labor discovers that his "matter" can only be handled in a novel form. But even these so-called "problems" are not problems in the same sense that a technological problem, controlled by conditions of an objective nature publicly definable prior to the solution, is said to be a problem.

What has been said agrees only in part with Croce's doctrine that conception and expression are identical, because it recognizes that the activity of imagining takes place through and in a material medium which resists the artist's efforts, and without intimate familiarity with which no purely mental imagining would be possible to him. To suppose, however, that the creative process is a hit-and-miss matter of following the suggestions which the medium somehow originates, is either to give evidence of complete ignorance of the creative activity or of honorable but purely deductive loyalty to a theory irrespective of easily available facts.

The reason for this discussion is the need to point out the complexity of the creative process by showing how notions of simple problem solving, particularly of the behaviorally observable type, fail to account for the way in which matter taken in by the senses is literally added to while it is also to some extent merely reshuffled. It indicates a purely external and inadequate knowledge of what is involved to assume that creative activity consists merely of the reshuffling of discrete elements or of atomic contents and experienced forms into other combinations. The product of the creative mind is not a mere combination, but a *creation* in a sense that no behaviorist or mechanist can admit and remain true to his theories. Creative activity takes place very rarely; but when it takes place it adds something new to the content of experience.

There is, it would seem, very little excuse for contemporary naturalists to neglect the creative imagination in their view of mind, since Dewey has given it a prominent place in *Art as Experience*.[7] Dewey acknowledges that the artist produces something *new*—and as I read him, he means something literally new, since the product of the creative imagination goes beyond the forms and matter received from without and thus involves an addition to the fund of informed meanings that are brought to the act of composition. As against the tradition headed by Hobbes, which virtually denies the active imagination, Dewey takes his position with the idealists who, with Leibnitz, assert that there is nothing in the mind that does not come through the senses—*except the mind itself*. The content of experience is not merely shuffled by the poet but is transformed and transsubstanced. He advances on what he takes in; he does not merely recombine his funded meanings ingeniously into patterns that have themselves been suggested by shuffling experience. The issue of such a process of mere shuffling is mechanical and imitative: but art does not imitate nature; instead it breaks up its meanings and forms, so to speak, under the impact of experience, and then fuses the whole into something utterly new.

This is not the place to ask how Dewey reconciles his recognition of the spontaneity of the mind with his naturalism; it is enough for us to point out that his account of the creative activity makes nonsense of the universal applicability of the scientific method. Nor is it the place to ask how he reconciles what he says about the creative mind's activity with his antipathy toward introspection. Dewey's book on aesthetics (which in many respects seems to me to be the least instrumentalistic of his books and to contain therefore the soundest part of his philosophy) is referred to in order to make concretely an important point: namely, that the genuine and first-hand interest in one of the important activities of the human spirit forced him to take seriously the spontaneity of the mind, thus leading him to transcend, at one point at least, the limitations inherent in his scientistic methodolatry.

It may be retorted that the assumption of spontaneity blocks inquiry —we should try to get at the possible determinations that control the creative act, the search for which it is wise to encourage. To this criticism two replies, at least, should be made. The first is that this is a counsel of perfection prompted by a narrow scientistic interest which would interdict all aesthetic speculation until the glorious *mañana* when be-

---

[7] John Dewey, *Art as Experience* (New York: Minton, Balch & Company, 1934), p. 70 *et passim*.

haviorists will give us an adequate theory of the creative artist. The second reply is that it was Dewey himself, whose philosophy was proclaimed by one of the contributors to Krikorian's volume as "the vanguard of twentieth century naturalism," [8] who recognized the spontaneity of the mind, and that his recognition was based on close empirical, although not "scientific," analysis of the aesthetic activity. "Spontaneity" is indeed Dewey's own word, and not one merely attributed by the writer to him. And while the writer is in hearty agreement with Dewey in his emphasis on the creative contribution of the mind in the poetic process, it is for the latter, who is a naturalist, and not for the writer, that the recognition constitutes a problem. One of the reasons the writer had to abandon the naturalistic doctrines which he once defended is that he was forced to recognize the mind's spontaneity, an insight to which he was led in part by the study of Dewey's aesthetics. Once you grasp the importance of the mind's spontaneity you can easily see how naïve and simplistic are the efforts of scientists when they try to reduce it to processes of reshuffling with which scientific method can deal. If the scientist must ignore what he cannot observe and measure, let him do so—but why, except as prompted by doctrinaire intransigence, must he deny that which eludes him?

A theory of mind that does not take into consideration the phenomenon of the creative imagination, or that reduces it to complex mechanical reshuffling and anticipatory manipulation, is not a theory of what is distinctive and of chief interest about the human mind to one interested in the genuine values of the human spirit. And if some of us will grant that the only real value of the best explanations of the creative activity now available consists in their revealing the complexity of the problem and thus in a sense of mystifying further what is already mysterious enough, the moral of our admission is not that a naturalistic theory of mind has succeeded where other theories have failed, for the opposite is the case; but that so long as such a phenomenon remains unexplained, naturalists have no ground for the militant and intransigent faith they express in their philosophy. If what they are interested in is the advancement of the truth and not the propagation of a doctrinaire philosophy, the least that can be expected of them is that they admit the limitations and inadequacies of their theories and their method. No service is done science or philosophy by attempting to claim for a doctrine or a method a virtue that it does not have. The sanguine assumption that in the

[8] *Naturalism, op. cit.,* p. 183.

future the creative activity will be understood scientifically is no ground
for affirming that at present the methods of scientific psychology are
applicable to it. Until they are successfully applied, the naturalistic
philosopher's confidence puts one in mind of the little boy who, having
borrowed the salt-shaker from his harrassed mother, proudly proclaimed
that he had captured the bird.

CREATIVITY IN ART

VINCENT TOMAS

When a rifleman aims at his target, he knows what he wants to do. He wants to hit the bull's-eye. Before he shoots, he knows what the target is; he knows that the black circle in the center of it is the bull's-eye; and he knows that hitting the bull's-eye consists in causing a bullet to pass through that black circle. He also knows, before he has squeezed the trigger, that if, after he has squeezed it, a hole appears in the black circle, he will have succeeded in doing what he wanted to do; and that if there isn't a hole there, he will have failed.

Furthermore, the rifleman knows what he ought to do to hit the bull's-eye. He knows what position he ought to assume, how he ought to adjust the sling, where exactly he ought to place his left hand, where he ought to place the butt so that it fits his shoulder and cheek, what the sight picture ought to be, how he ought to exhale a little and then

From The Philosophical Review, *Vol. LXVII, No. 1 (1958). Reprinted by permission of the editors of* The Philosophical Review.

hold his breath when the sight picture is correct, and how he ought to squeeze off the shot without knowing exactly when the explosion will come, so that he won't flinch until after it is too late to spoil his aim.

If, after the rifleman has attempted to obey all these rules, he fails to hit the bull's-eye, any sergeant can tell him, and the rifleman will agree, that he did fail; and that, since he did, he had not obeyed all the rules. For, if he had obeyed them, there necessarily would have been a hole in the bull's-eye. If, on the other hand, he does hit the bull's-eye, the white disc is displayed and the rifleman is congratulated. He is congratulated, whether the people who congratulate him realize it or not, for having been able to learn and to obey all the rules.

When we congratulate an artist for being creative, however, it is not because he was able to obey rules that were known before he painted his picture or wrote his novel or poem, so that thereby he succeeded in doing what had been done before. We congratulate him because he embodied in colors or in language something the like of which did not exist before, and because he was the originator of the rules he implicitly followed while he was painting or writing. Afterwards, others may *explicitly* follow the same rules and thereby achieve similar successes. But the academic painter or writer is like the rifleman. He, too, aims at a known target, and he hits his bull's-eye by obeying known rules. As Sir Joshua Reynolds wrote:

> By studying carefully the works of great masters, this advantage is obtained; we find that certain niceties of expression are capable of being executed, which otherwise we might suppose beyond the reach of art. This gives us a confidence in ourselves; and we are thus incited to endeavor at not only the same happiness of execution, but also at other congenial excellencies. Study indeed consists in learning to see nature, and may be called the art of using other men's minds.[1]

Unlike either the rifleman or the academic painter or writer, the creative artist does not initially know what his target is. Although he seems to himself to be "aiming" at something, it is not until just before he affixes his signature or seal of approval to his work that he finds out that *this* is the determinate thing he was all along "aiming" at, and that *this* was the way to bring it into being. Creative activity in art, that is to say, is not a paradigm of purposive activity, that is, of activity engaged in and consciously controlled so as to produce a desired result.

---

[1] From a fragment. Published in Elizabeth Gilmore Holt, *Literary Sources of Art History* (Princeton: Princeton University Press, 1947), p. 504.

In the paradigmatic case, the agent envisages the result he desires to produce and has it consciously in view, and he believes that if he acts in certain ways the result desired will be produced. Although we may say that his activity is "teleologically controlled," to explain it we do not appeal to a final cause, but only to an efficient cause, namely, to his desire for the result he envisages and his beliefs. But when he is impelled to engage in creative activity, the artist, as has been said, does not already envisage the final result. He does not therefore already have an idea or image of it. And his activity therefore is not "controlled," as in the paradigm case, by a desire for an envisaged result and beliefs about how to obtain it.

If, however, creative activity differs from clear-cut cases of purposive activity in the ways mentioned, it resembles purposive activity in other ways. As has been said, the creative artist has a sense that his activity is directed—that it is heading somewhere. Now the cash value of the statement that the artist has a sense of being engaged in a directed activity, of going somewhere despite the fact that he cannot say precisely where he is going while he is still on the way, is that he *can* say that certain directions are not right. After writing a couplet or drawing a line, he will erase it because it is "wrong" and try again. If there were in him no tendency to go in a certain direction, he would not resist being pulled in just any direction. This element of conscious resistance to the lure of beckoning side paths, or the exercise of critical judgment, is what sets creative activity apart from activity that is acquiescent to the leadership of revery. In the latter, anything goes and nothing is rejected. Here we ought not to say that nothing is rejected because everything that the imagination suggests is consented to as "right," but only that all is accepted without criticism. Coleridge and the idealists were correct, therefore, in so far as they distinguished creative activity from the exercise of passive imagination, or fancy. Essential to the former, while absent from the latter, are critical judgment and fastidiousness.

Creative activity in art, then, is activity subject to critical control by the artist, although not by virtue of the fact that he foresees the final result of the activity. That this way of construing creativity reflects part of what we have in mind when we speak of creative art can be shown if we contrast what results from creative activity so construed with what results from other activities that we do not call creative.

Thus we do not judge a painting, poem, or other work to be a work of creative art unless we believe it to be original. If it strikes us as being a repetition of other paintings or poems, if it seems to be the result of a mechanical application of a borrowed technique or style to novel subject matter, to the degree that we apprehend it as such, to the same degree we deny that it is creative. There are men who have trained themselves to paint in the manner of Rembrandt, and some have become so good at it that even an expert aided by X-rays may find it hard to decide that their pictures were *not* painted by Rembrandt. Whatever other merits we attribute to such a painter or to his work, we do not judge him to be creative. He is like the rifleman. He knows what his bull's-eye is, and he knows how to hit it. Even in the case of a painter who has created a style of his own, we do not say that he is creating his style when he is painting his thirtieth or fortieth picture in that style. We may judge the style to be a good one, and the painting as a whole to be good. Yet we will grant that with respect to style the painter is no longer creative but is only repeating himself. To create is to originate. And it follows from this that prior to creation the creator does not foresee what will result from it. As T. E. Hulme put it, "to predict it would be to produce it before it was produced." [2]

Hulme's remark may sound odd, but it really isn't. To predict the result of his creative activity, the artist would have to envisage that result. He would have to have the idea of it in mind. But if he already had the idea in mind, all that would remain to be done is to objectify the idea in paint or in stone, and this would be a matter of skill, or work. That is why sculptors who do not need to work their material before they can envisage the determinate statue they want to make, but who can describe exactly what it should be like before the first blow of the mallet is struck, often hire stone-cutters to execute their plan. By the time they have the idea, the creative act, which in this case is the production of the idea, is finished. But to produce that original idea, the sculptor does not first have to produce an idea of it.

Although we do not judge a work to be a work of creative art unless we believe it to be original, it is not enough that we should judge it to be merely different or novel. In discourse about art, we use "creative" in an honorific sense, in a sense in which creative activity always issues in something that is different in an interesting, important, fruitful, or other *valuable* way. If what the artist produces is a novelty, yet indifferent or bad, we do not regard him as a creator. It is granted that, as R. G. Collingwood points out, there is a sense of the word in which we

---

[2] "Speculations," in *The Problem of Aesthetics,* Eliseo Vivas and Murray Krieger, eds. (New York: Holt, Rinehart & Winston, Inc., 1953), p. 126.

say that a man creates a nuisance or a disturbance. Yet if we believe, for example, that all that the Dadaists "created" was a nuisance and a disturbance, we will not judge them to have been creative artists.

Since "creative" as applied to art has this honorific sense, we will tend not to apply the term to any activity which does not result in a product having positive aesthetic or artistic value. To the degree that a work lacks coherence and lucidity, to the degree that it is not a unified whole the relations between whose parts are felt by aesthetic intuition as necessary, not fortuitous, connections, to that degree it will fail to be a work of creative art. Now a reason or ground for a judgment that something is not a work of creative art, I suggest, is not merely that the work as we see it lacks coherence and lucidity. Rather, this lack in the work is taken as evidence of a lack of control by the artist over the activity to which the work owes its origin, or of coherence and lucidity in him. And if this were so, then what he produced would not be a work of creative art. This is why, I suggest, we distinguish works of creative art from products of passive imagination on the one hand, and from the art of the insane on the other.

To illustrate the sort of works that we can expect to be produced under the guidance of passive imagination, I will use two extreme examples. These were deliberately chosen because of their bearing on a theory of artistic creativity, one thesis of which is that "Poetic creation, like the dream, is governed by strict psychic laws." [3]

In 1823, Ludwig Börne published an essay entitled "The Art of Becoming an Original Writer in Three Days." According to Ernest Jones, it was his reading of this essay that gave Sigmund Freud his "trust in the validity of free associations." [4] Börne writes:

> Here follows the practical prescription I promised. Take a few sheets of paper and for three days in succession write down, without any falsification or hypocrisy, everything that comes into your head. Write what you think of yourself, of your women, of the Turkish war, of Goethe, of the Fonk criminal case, of the Last Judgment, of those senior to you in authority—and when the three days are over you will be amazed at what novel and startling thoughts have welled up in you. That is the art of becoming an original writer in three days. [5]

---

[3] A. Bronson Feldman, "Reik and the Interpretation of Literature," *Explorations in Psychoanalysis*, Robert Lindner and Clement Staff, eds. (New York: The Julian Press, Inc., 1953), p. 103.

[4] *The Life and Works of Sigmund Freud*, Vol. I (New York: Basic Books, Inc., 1953), p. 245. See also p. 246.

[5] *Ibid.*, p. 246.

No doubt someone who follows this prescription will, when the three days are over, be amazed when he reads what novel and startling things he has written. And it is not impossible that some of the statements will be judged by him to be adequate formulations of what he thinks—of himself, of his women, of Goethe, or of the Last Judgment, difficult subjects every one of them about which most of us don't know what we think unless, by a creative act, as distinguished from free association, we have found out. But it is much more probable that what was so written would be rejected by the writer as an inadequate expression of his thought. In any case, if everything were left exactly as it was just because it happened to come into the writer's head, we would not take it seriously as creative literature. Rather, to borrow another quotation from Reynolds, we would say, "When [the] desire of novelty has proceeded from mere idleness or caprice, it is not worth the trouble of criticism." [6]

The second horrible example is drawn from an essay in many ways similar to the one by Ludwig Börne. It is by Alva Johnston and the title is "How to Become a Great Writer." [7] Virtually all of this essay is the biography of a great writer. Johnston tells of a young man who, as Freud says of the artist, like other men longed "to attain to honor, power, riches, fame, and the love of women," [8] but to whom reality denied all these things. After graduating from a university, full of ambition, he accepted a job which he soon gave up in favor of another, paying less money but offering better prospects. The prospects proved to be illusory, so he changed jobs again, drawn by further illusory prospects. This was repeated several times. After some years he found himself burdened with a family and with an income smaller than his allowance as a student had been. Goaded by frustration, he did not take to drink but instead indulged in ritualistic daydreaming. For some years he devoted an hour each day to spinning castles in the air, and by inhabiting them in the role of hero he achieved a make-believe gratification of his desires. One day, when he was returning home, he bought a pulp magazine and read one of the stories. This opened his eyes. That evening, instead of daydreaming, he sat down with some sheets of paper and began to write one of his phantasies down. What he wrote was rejected by an extraordinary number of publishers. They

[6] "Discourses," in Holt, op. cit., p. 510.

[7] Saturday Evening Post, July 29, 1939 (Vol. 212, No. 5, pp. 5-7, 58-60).

[8] A General Introduction to Psychoanalysis, Joan Riviere, trans. (New York: Liveright Publishing Corporation, 1935), p. 327.

gave such reasons as that the setting lacked authenticity, the style was atrocious, and the plot was infantile. But at length the manuscript was accepted and published, and the book proved to be a tremendous commercial success. By 1939 it and its sequels had sold thirty million copies and had been translated into fifty-six languages; and the author was living in a luxurious mansion in the Southwest. Thus he had won, as Freud says, "through his phantasy—what before he could win only in phantasy: honor, power, and the love of women." [9] The name of the writer is Edgar Rice Burroughs, and the title of his first book is *Tarzan of the Apes*.[10]

Its being subject to critical control sets creative art apart not only from the sort of thing just described, but from the art of the insane. There is an ancient tradition that the creative artist is a man possessed. To give once more the familiar quotations from Plato:

> For the poet is a light and winged and holy thing, and there is no invention in him until he has been inspired and is out of his senses, and the mind is no longer in him: when he has not attained to this state, he is powerless and is unable to utter his oracles [*Ion*, 534].
> But he who, having no touch of the Muses' madness in his soul, comes to the door and thinks that he will get into the temple by the help of art—he, I say, and his poetry are not admitted; the sane man disappears and is nowhere when he enters into rivalry with the madman [*Phaedrus*, 245].

Shakespeare says:

> The lunatic, the lover, and the poet
> Are of imagination all compact.
> [*Midsummer Night's Dream*, V, i]

Despite this impressive tradition, we cannot accept the view that creative artists must literally be madmen. The pictures they paint and the poetry they write make sense, whereas this is not true of the art of the insane. When we gaze in succession upon a series of pictures by psychotics, we see that in them all there is a note of nightmare, delirium, or mania which is not present in, for instance, da Vinci's drawings of monsters or even in surrealist paintings. The difference may be described by saying that in the surrealist painting, delusion or nightmare

---

[9] *Ibid.*, p. 328.
[10] Johnston, who was writing a popular article, makes no mention of Freud. But it is worth remarking that, if his account is accurate, Burroughs is a perfect case study in support of what Freud said about artists in "The Relation of the Poet to Daydreaming" (1908) and elsewhere. Ernst Kris is the only Freudian writer on art I have read who is not blind to the distinction between creative and noncreative art.

is portrayed or objectified, whereas no matter what an insane man portrays or objectifies—be it "Mother" or "God"—his psychosis is revealed. If the art of the insane makes sense to us, it is in the manner of a sign or symptom of psychosis, not in the manner of an expression of it.

Here it may occur to the reader to raise the question of Van Gogh, whose later works, we may suppose, are works of creative art, but in which there is a kind of stridency signifying madness. The answer, I suggest, is that it is only in so far as there is more in them than a stridency signifying madness that we regard them as products of creative art. Those paintings were not done, that is to say, in the complete absence of conscious control and criticism. In psychiatric language, which I borrow from Ernst Kris, those paintings were not completely tied to Van Gogh's delusional system. As Kris says, in Van Gogh, "the disorder manifests itself in a change of style, but even though the style has changed, the connections with the artistic tendencies of the individual and his environment are preserved." [11]

Creativity and madness have traditionally been associated mainly though not entirely because of the phenomenon of inspiration. In the creative process, two moments may be distinguished, the moment of inspiration, when the new suggestion appears in consciousness, and the moment of development or elaboration. The moment of inspiration is sometimes accompanied by exalted feelings, and this is why, according to Charles Lamb, it is confused with madness. According to Lamb,

> men, finding in the raptures of the higher poetry a condition of exaltation, to which they have no parallel in their own experience, besides the spurious resemblance of it in dreams and fevers, impute a state of dreaminess and fever to the poet. But the true poet dreams being awake. He is not possessed by his subject but has dominion over it.[12]

The "moment" of development may last a long time, of course, even years. During that more or less long moment the artist is striving to find out what his inspiration is. As in the cases of Flaubert and of Hemingway, he may write and rewrite and hone and polish until at last he can look upon what he has done and say, "There! That's what I wanted to say, just as I wanted to say it." Before that, he knew only that what he had so far done was *not* quite what he wanted to say, or quite how he wanted to say it. It seems obvious that Flaubert, during

---

[11] *Psychoanalytic Explorations in Art* (New York: International Universities Press, Inc., 1952), p. 94.

[12] "The Sanity of True Genius," *The Works of Charles and Mary Lamb*, Vol. II, E. V. Lucas, ed. (New York: G. P. Putnam's Sons, 1903), p. 187.

that long moment of elaboration during which he fashioned *Madame Bovary,* was critically controlling what he was doing. He was neither mad nor free-associating nor spinning daydreams. However, as Plato reminds us, if Flaubert had had no touch of the Muses' madness in his soul, there would have been no invention in him. He would have had no inspiration and therefore nothing to elaborate. In that case, however long he wrote and rewrote, honed and polished, nothing would have come of it.

Now inspiration, so far as we know, is not subject to our will. We cannot decide to have an inspiration, nor can we by reasoning conclude our way into it. And if by "art" we mean, as Plato did, skill—an activity consciously controlled so as to produce an already envisaged result— then art is not enough to produce an inspiration. When, therefore, Plato says that "there is no invention in him until he has become inspired and is out of his senses, and the mind is no longer in him"; or when he says, "he who, having no touch of the Muses' madness in his soul, comes to the door and thinks that he will get into the temple by the help of art—he, I say, and his poetry are not admitted," he may mean what I have just said, though he says it in a less prosaic way. If he does mean that inspiration is necessary for creative art, and that it is not by reasoning or by the exercise of skill that artists become inspired, we may agree. At the same time we should observe that this does not entail that when an artist has been inspired he becomes incapable of exercising skill in developing his inspiration, or that reason in the sense of a capacity for critical control "is no longer in him," or that the artist is literally a "madman."

Here it may be objected that cases of dramatically sudden and apparently fully determinate inspiration are being left out of the account, cases such as the one Nietzsche describes in *Ecce Homo* in the following words:

> something profoundly convulsive and disturbing suddenly becomes visible and audible with indescribable definiteness and exactness. One hears—one does not seek; one takes—one does not ask who gives. . . . There is the feeling that one is utterly out of hand. . . . Everything occurs without volition. . . . The spontaneity of the images and similes is most remarkable. . . . If I may borrow a phrase of Zarathustra's, it actually seems as if the things themselves came to one, and offered themselves as similes.[18]

[18] *The Philosophy of Nietzsche* (New York: Modern Library, Inc., n.d.), pp. 896f.

In such cases, the two moments of inspiration and elaboration collapse into one, and the poem issues forth in the complete absence of critical control. Or so it would seem. It is such cases that lend support to such truth as there is in the view that the creative artist is out of his mind, and in the Romanticist theory that art is the spontaneous overflow of powerful feelings. But was the manner in which Nietzsche wrote *Thus Spake Zarathustra* completely blind and automatic, or was there after all some critical control? I submit that there probably was. My reasons for thinking that there probably was may perhaps not have very much weight; but I am inclined to think they have some weight—the weight of common sense.

C. S. Peirce refers to a man who, when he was asked what he thought of the fact that the sun obeyed Joshua's command to stand still, replied, "Well, I'll bet that the sun wiggled just a bit when no one was looking." Similarly, I'll bet that Nietzsche edited just a bit while he wrote down *Thus Spake Zarathustra*. Should we accept reports of fully determinate inspiration at their face value as being about cases in which the moving finger writes, and, having writ, moves on? Is it absurd to suspect that such cases are in fact more like the parody of Omar's famous line?

> The moving finger writes, and having writ
> Moves on. But lo! It stops a bit.
> Moves back to cross a T, insert a word.
> The moving finger's acting quite absurd.

Even if Nietzsche didn't deliberately change a thing, even if all came out just right from the very first line, was there not a relatively cool hour when Nietzsche (and the same goes for Coleridge and *Kubla Kahn*) read what he had written and judged it to be an adequate expression of his thought? Haven't we all had the experience of being seized by the Muse in the middle of the night and writing as if possessed, only to read what we had written the next morning and to consign it not to a publisher but to the wastebasket?

If there was such a cool hour and such a critical judgment in Nietzsche's case, this is all that is needed to have made him create *Zarathustra* on the view of creation presented above. C. J. Ducasse has stated the point precisely in his *The Philosophy of Art*. Ducasse writes:

> To say that art is conscious . . . or . . . critically controlled . . . does not mean that it need be conscious or so controlled either antecedently to or contemporaneously with the expressive act. . . . But it does mean that *a critical judgment is an intrinsic, essential constituent of the productive activity called art;* and indeed, not

merely a critical judgment, but a *favorable* one. . . . One must be able to acknowledge the product as an adequate statement of one-self. . . . The telic character, which truly belongs to art since a critical moment is an intrinsic part of it, may be said to accrue to the expressive activity which is its first moment ex post facto. That activity is telically construed and criticized *after* it has occurred. And the work of art is not the product of that activity simply, but of that activity telically construed and criticized, and if need be repeated until correction of the product results, i.e., until objectivity of the expression is obtained.[14]

Given the concepts of conscious critical control and inspiration, we are in a position, I think, to set aside certain theories about creativity in art. Whether this can be done, by the way, should be of interest not only to philosophers of art but to metaphysicians and others as well.

Eliseo Vivas, in *Creation and Discovery,* finds in artistic creativity a difficulty for any "naturalistic" theory of mind. According to Vivas, what a naturalistic theory has to explain, but so far cannot explain, is

the control that the new whole, which from the standpoint of con-sciousness has not yet been fully born, exercises over the artist's mind as he proceeds to bring it to birth. . . . [We need to ex-plain] the purposive thrust of the mind, the mind's ability to follow the lead of something which is not pushing it from behind, so to speak, since it is not-yet-there. It is this fact, the control of the not-yet-there total situation over the present, that leads the idealist to insist that a factor is here at work of an essentially teleological nature.[15]

When the problem is formulated in this way, we are asked to explain how artistic creation is guided or controlled by an object that is "not-yet-there," that is, by something that does not exist, since it has not yet been created. And we may be tempted to say that, since it exercises an influence, the to-be-created object *is,* somehow, "there." It is an ideal or subsistent object which, perhaps in the manner of Aristotle's Prime Mover, does not push the artist's mind from behind, but attracts it from in front. It is, that is to say, not a kick, but a carrot, which the artist follows until the subsistent object stands revealed to him. Hence, crea-tion is discovery.

But what needs to be explained is not, as Vivas formulates it, "the control that the new whole exercises over the artist's mind as he pro-ceeds to bring it to birth." What needs to be explained is the fact that creative activity is controlled, but not by virtue of the fact that the artist

---

[14] New York: The Dial Press, Inc., 1929, pp. 115f.
[15] New York: Noonday Press, 1955, pp. 151f.

already envisages the result he will create. That the artist's choices are controlled by a whole that is not-yet-there is not a fact but a theory. On the alternative theory that has been presented in this paper, what control consists in is the making of critical judgments about what has so far been done. There may be a great many of these judgments or, in the limiting cases, just one.

But how, when he makes his critical judgments, does the artist know what is right and what is wrong? On the alternative theory, he knows because there is something pushing him from behind. Whenever the artist goes wrong, he feels himself being kicked, and he tries another way which, he surmises, trusts, or hopes, will not be followed by a kick. What is kicking him is "inspiration," which is already there. What he makes must be adequate to his inspiration. If it isn't, he feels a kick. We have all felt similar kicks when we have tried to put into words something we mean that we have not formulated before. On many such occasions, and they are always occasions on which we are *listening* to what we are saying as well as talking, we have uttered a sentence and then withdrawn it because it did not express what we meant, and we have sought to substitute for it another sentence which did.

Admittedly, the concept of inspiration we have been making use of is in need of clarification. Fortunately, it is not essential to our present purpose to attempt this task, since no matter whether the inspiration that appears at the threshold of the artist's reflexive consciousness is an impression, an emotion, a phantasy, an unclear idea, or whatnot, it is something that is "already there" in the creative process. That it should be already there is, for our purpose, the essential point.

In conclusion, let us consider briefly the view that when the moment of inspiration is distinct from the more or less long moment of its development or elaboration, during this second moment the mind of the artist is directed by his apprehension of "aesthetic necessity."

According to Brand Blanshard,

Invention turns on a surrender to the workings of necessity in one's mind. [There is in the artist] a surrender of the will to an order whose structure is quite independent of it and whose affirmation through the mind is very largely so.[16]

---

[16] *The Nature of Thought,* Vol. II (New York: The Macmillan Company, 1940), pp. 139, 166.

In writing the last act of *Othello,* Blanshard continues, Shakespeare wrote what he did

> for the same reason that we, in reading or hearing it, find it satis-
> fying, namely that with the given dramatic situation in mind "he
> could no other.". . . Given the character of Othello, his prevailing
> mood, his habits of speech, the situation in which he was placed, and
> given the need to round out the whole in accordance with the im-
> plicit demands of the aesthetic ideal, there was only one course for
> the Moor to take; and that he did.[17]

On this view, when an artist is inspired, what is given to him is analogous to a set of postulates and definitions in logic or mathematics; and what he does when he develops his inspiration is analogous to what a logician does when he deduces theorems from the postulates. Another analogy which is sometimes used is that inspiration is like an acorn. If the artist is inspired by an acorn, he can nurture it properly and develop an oak; or he may nurture it improperly and develop a stunted oak; but he can by no means develop an elm.

Such analogies, while they express how it feels to the artist when he is creating, can I believe be very misleading, especially when they lead us to postulate an ideal order of aesthetic necessity. Granted that we intuit "aesthetic necessity" in works of art, a lot of missing premises must be supplied before we can conclude that artistic creation is in important respects similar to logical deduction. When searching for these premises, we do well to tread warily.

For instance, from the fact that we feel (assuming that we do so feel) that the last act of *Othello* perfectly coheres with the preceding acts, it does not follow that a different last act, in which the Moor takes a different course, would not also be felt to cohere with them. With a different last act, we should have a different play, to be sure; but it might be an equally coherent one. Someone acquainted with it, and not with the play that we have, might well say about it that given the pre-ceding acts, there was in the last act "only one course for the Moor to take; and that he did."

If this possibility is denied, what is the reason for the denial? The reason cannot be, "Aesthetic necessity is like logical necessity," since that is the thesis at issue.

---

[17] *Ibid.,* p. 145.

SELECTED
BIBLIOGRAPHY

Alexander, Samuel, *Beauty and Other Forms of Value,* Chap. 4. London: Macmillan & Co., Ltd., 1933.

Bergson, Henri, *Laughter.* New York: Doubleday & Company, Inc., 1956.

Blanshard, Brand, *The Nature of Thought,* Vol. II, Chaps. 23-24. London: George Allen & Unwin, 1939.

Centeno, Augusto, ed., *The Intent of the Artist.* Princeton: Princeton University Press, 1941.

Croce, Benedetto, *Aesthetic as Science of Expression and General Linguistic,* Part I. New York: The Noonday Press, 1956.

Dewey, John, *Art as Experience,* Chap. 4. New York: Minton, Balch & Company, 1934.

Freud, Sigmund, "The Relation of the Poet to Day-Dreaming," *Collected Papers,* Vol. IV. London: Hogarth Press, Ltd., 1925.

Hausman, Carl R., "Mechanism and Teleology in the Creative Process," *The Journal of Philosophy,* Vol. LVIII (1961).

James, Henry, *The Art of the Novel,* pp. 119-125. New York: Charles Scribner's Sons, 1934.

Langer, Susanne K., *Feeling and Form,* Part II. New York: Charles Scribner's Sons, 1953.

Maritain, Jacques, *Creative Intuition in Art and Poetry.* New York: Pantheon Books, Inc., 1953.

Morgan, Douglas, "Creativity Today," *Journal of Aesthetics and Art Criticism,* Vol. XII (1953).